Going Graphic
Comics at Work in the Multilingual Classroom

Stephen Cary

Heinemann ■ ■ ■ Portsmouth, NH

Heinemann
A division of Reed Elsevier Inc.
361 Hanover Street
Portsmouth, NH 03801–3912
www.heinemann.com

Offices and agents throughout the world

© 2004 by Stephen Cary

Library of Congress Cataloging-in-Publication Data
Cary, Stephen, 1946–
Going graphic : comics at work in the multilingual classroom / Stephen Cary.
   p.   cm.
   Includes bibliographical references and index.
   ISBN 0-325-00475-7 (alk. paper)
   1. English language—Study and teaching—Foreign speakers—Audio-visual aids.   2. Second language acquisition—Audio-visual aids.   3. Comic books, strips, etc. in education.   I. Title.
PE1128.A2C36 2004
428′.0071—dc22   2004009979

EDITOR: *Lois Bridges*
PRODUCTION: *Elizabeth Valway*
COVER DESIGN: *Catherine Hawkes, Cat and Mouse*
INTERIOR DESIGN: *Jenny Jensen Greenleaf*
COMPOSITION: *Technologies 'N Typography*
MANUFACTURING: *Steve Bernier*

Printed in the United States of America on acid-free paper
08 07 06 05 04 EB 1 2 3 4 5

For
Mom and Dad,
the real deal in superheroes

Contents

Acknowledgments

A big thanks . . .

To the teachers and students who field-tested the comics activities and shared their ideas and insights with me.

To the artists and publishers who kindly donated artwork.

To Joe Field, owner of Flying Colors Comics in Concord, California, for information on the comics industry, guidance on materials—and all those freebies!

To Trina Robbins, women's comics pioneer and historian, for her gracious help with artist contacts.

To ARBMS for the patience and the nuzzling while I lived in Writing Land.

And finally, a special thanks to Lois Bridges, my editor at Heinemann, for "getting" comics, championing the book, and supporting me from start to finish with such competence, grace, and good humor.

Introduction

Hooked on Comics

Superman made me a reader. Dick and Jane tried their best, but they couldn't give me what The Man of Steel offered: a good reason to read. Like most American school kids in the 1950s, I learned the reading fundamentals through basal readers and workbooks. I did my round-robin reading, expanded my stock of sight words, and picked up an assortment of word attack skills. I could decode and comprehend like a champ, but I had little to no interest in what teachers were asking me to read.

Reading became a deadly bore and, by extension, school too, since reading was such a large part of what went on in school. I could read, but I hated reading, and by the fourth grade I'd become the classic nonreading reader. Fifteen minutes alone with a book was better than having my tonsils out, but not by much. I read only what I had to read in school. Away from school, I built model cars and planes, collected stamps and coins, played baseball, and periodically set the house on fire with my chemistry set. But I didn't read, wouldn't read.

Superman flew into my life in 1956 and changed everything. My dad had taken a part-time job distributing magazines and comics to newsstands and drugstores around Omaha, Nebraska, and as a job perk, he could grab what he wanted from the company's remainder piles. He grabbed Astounding Science Fiction and Ellery Queen mystery mags for himself and Mom, and comic books for his nonreading son.

I was immediately hooked. Comics had the art, color, movement, and raw energy missing from my school reading. Best of all, I liked the stories and cared about the characters. I never once wanted to be any of the people I read about in school. But I would have changed places with Superman or Batman or Turok, Son of Stone, in an instant.

For a ten-year-old, the wild and refreshingly improbable stories, the superpowered heroes, the ruthless villains, the silliness and slapstick, and that extraordinary march of drawings across the page, like a slow-motion movie cartoon where you could savor each frame as long as you wished, were pure magic.

The Taboo of Choice

I devoured every comic book I could get my hands on through middle school and into my first year of high school, including all the Classics Illustrated like *The Three Musketeers* and *A Tale of Two Cities*. I'd become a reader—someone who read, rather than simply someone who could read—through comics, not through school. And in fact, school did everything it could to squelch my comic book reading. Most teachers banned them from the classroom, believing them frivolous and educationally bankrupt at best, lurid and morally unhealthy at worst. Mrs. Dixon, my fifth-grade teacher, would seize any comic she spotted in the classroom, wave the offending title high above her head, and declare it a cheap, worthless read before impounding it till the end of time in one of her desk drawers.

Comic book reading was one of the great school taboos, along with smoking, fighting, and swearing, and that made comics even more appealing to me and my comics-crazed friends. None of us smoked or fought, and none of us swore with any authority, so by default, comics became the taboo of choice. We loaded up on Green Arrow, Wonder Woman, Uncle Scrooge, The Flash, and dozens of other titles, collected comics, traded comics, talked comics, lived comics, and read them like there was no tomorrow. As a sophomore, I set comics aside and moved on to sci-fi novels, historical fiction, and true-life adventure tales with the same drive that had carried me through those hundreds of superhero and Disney comics only a few years earlier.

Comics in a Second Language

By the early seventies, I'd started reading comics again, this time in my second language instead of my first and, as before, in spite of school, not because of it. College Spanish was killing me. I was drowning in page after page, book after book, of dense, mostly incomprehensible text. I used a bilingual dictionary to look up a good dozen words a page, but still wasn't really understanding what I was reading. Early reading in Spanish was as tiresome as early reading in English—and a lot more painful.

A summer trip to Mexico opened my eyes on the second language and second culture fronts. I found comics widely available, widely read, and amazingly, given my experiences with comics provincialism in the United States, read by both kids and adults. I bought armloads of Kalimán, La Familia Burrón, and my old favorite, Supermán, ¡El Héroe de Metrópolis!, and dove in, suddenly swimming rather than sinking in Spanish reading. The visuals reduced the amount of written text I had to tackle and provided comprehension clues that made learning Spanish vocabulary and structures easier. I was also picking up colloquialisms and pop culture knowledge I could immediately put to use in my Mexican travels. For the first time, second language reading was fun, manageable, and best of all, useful.

By the mid-seventies, I was teaching second language learners in the California public schools and making comics a key ingredient in our SSR (Sustained Silent Reading) program, despite loud disapproval by a few comics-phobic colleagues. I visited the local thrift stores every few months and loaded up on comics. My sixth graders consumed tons of comics and comic strip books, reading them at school and then taking them home to read again or share with siblings. Students talked about the comics and wrote about the comics.

Firsthand, I saw students gaining second language with the help of Peanuts, Spider-Man, Archie, Betty and Veronica, and all the Looney Tunes crew. My students read more than comics, of course, but they did read a lot of comics, and some students, especially those at a beginning or early intermediate stage in English language proficiency, typically chose comics at free reading time. I understood the why of that in my bones; I had made the same choice during my free reading time in Mexico.

Later, as a resource teacher and administrator, I shared comics activities with receptive teachers, but those teachers were few and far between. Over the past dozen years, in my work as an educational consultant and university instructor, I've found more comics-friendly teachers, but comics-*using* teachers have remained scarce. Despite substantial research showing the benefits of reading comics (see Chapter 1), despite teachers' frequent calls for relevant, high-interest materials, and despite the fact that many teachers can't live without their daily dose of FoxTrot or Doonesbury, getting teachers to use comics is still a tough sell. But not an impossible sell. In fact, with some good, basic information and support, teachers take readily to comics.

Overview

This book gives teachers the knowledge and tools needed for using comics with second language learners. The instructional focus throughout is on the use of comics—cartoons, comic strips, comic books, and graphic novels—for both second language development and content learning. The book is pertinent to teachers working in elementary, secondary, and adult school settings and to students at all levels of second language proficiency.

Chapter 1 defines basic comics terms and offers a theoretical framework and research review that inform and support the use of comics in the multilingual classroom.

Chapter 2 uses a question-and-answer format to explore a host of issues confronting any teacher who includes comics in the curriculum. Issues run from program compatibility, content appropriateness, and boosting female readership, to material readability, variety, and the use of comics with reluctant readers. Along the way, the chapter dispels several long-standing myths about comics, quiets teachers' fears, and offers hints for sidestepping typical pitfalls.

Chapter 3 offers twenty-five communication-based activities that use comics across the grades and for a variety of language and content learning purposes. The activities integrate listening, speaking, reading, and writing, and feature a number of instructional approaches and strategies. Each activity includes detailed suggestions for implementation.

Finally, Chapter 4 serves as a mini–resource center where you can quickly locate materials for the book activities and those of your own design. You'll find comics reviews, publishers, how-to-draw books, comics-inspired films, and information on comics in languages other than English. Most important, the chapter lists websites where students can read thousands of comics online, including entire comic books.

Interwoven throughout the book are Field Sketches—anecdotes and insights from teachers and students around the United States and abroad who are using comics for second language development. The Field Sketches, coupled with personal reflections based on my work with hundreds of students and teachers over the past three decades, offer a close-up view of comics-in-action in the multilingual classroom.

Samples of commercial comics give readers a sense of the enormous range of material on the market, from wordless comics like Aragonés' Actions Speak and Otomo's text-reduced Akira, to Shanower's text-heavy and text-tough Age of Bronze series. Student samples show what second language learners at various grade levels can do—and learn—when given the opportunity to create their own comics.

English as a Second Language and Beyond

Though the book focuses primarily on developing English as a second language (ESL), all the activity ideas, strategies, and techniques, are applicable to any target language—Spanish, Vietnamese, Urdu, Nahuatl, or Klingon, and in both second and foreign language settings. A few of the suggested activities work better with students at a given proficiency level, but most work with all second language students, from square-one beginners to advanced learners. Moreover, with little and sometimes no modification, all the activities can be done with native English speakers as well.

This large-scale applicability is critical for teachers faced with the reality of the typical "too much–too many" classroom: too much curriculum, too many students, and never enough time for either. Teachers add comics to their program because the material helps them teach what they need to teach, and also helps them serve students with widely varying educational backgrounds and needs.

A Note on Terms

Two terms used repeatedly in the book merit definition: *second language learner (SLL)* and *multilingual classroom.* Second language learner here, given the book's ESL emphasis, usually refers to a student learning English as a second language. In a broader sense, however, a second language learner is any student who is learning another language beyond his first or primary language. The term, therefore, applies equally to Mandarin speakers learning English, English speakers learning Spanish, or Farsi speakers learning Swedish. The inclusive nature of the term contrasts dramatically with the parochialism of *English language learner (ELL),* a rival term that has gained in popularity over the past several years. English language learner, unlike SLL, conveys no hint of a student's existing primary language skills and her growing bilingualism. The term, whether intended or not, suggests a preference for linguistic assimilation over linguistic diversity—a native Spanish-speaking student, for example, on her way to becoming an English speaker, rather than a Spanish and English speaker.

The ELL term is also confusing as a student identifier, a label attempting to differentiate nonnative English speakers from native English speakers. The problem? All native English speakers are English language learners in North America, the British Isles, Australia, and New Zealand. I avoid the ELL term—in and out of the book—and stick with second language learner throughout.

The term *multilingual classroom* refers to any classroom with at least one or more second language learner students. The classroom can be at any grade level and in any public or private school setting. Though the term within these pages usually means a class with nonnative speakers learning English as a second language, it refers just as accurately to a foreign language classroom with native English speakers learning Russian, Japanese, Yoruba, or Dutch.

Getting the Most from the Book

All authors hope their book gets a cover-to-cover read. But anyone who writes for teachers and understands their time constraints can never reasonably expect it. When teachers dig into the professional literature, they quickly extract what they need to enhance curriculum and instruction and move on. This book is designed, then, with the time-strapped and always task-overwhelmed teacher in mind.

Each chapter stands on its own with several of the book's key ideas, such as the importance of high-interest content and teacher mediation in using comics, threading through each chapter. Feel free to read as many or as few chapters as you want. How many chapters you read will depend on the number of years you've taught, the size of your instructional bag of tricks, and most important, your experience using comics.

Veteran teachers, especially those who have worked with second language learners and are familiar with current second language acquisition (SLA) theory, might breeze past the theory and research chapter and some of the instructional strategy discussions and focus more on the activity ideas. Teachers new to second language learners will likely give theory and research much more time. Moreover, these sections will interest anyone needing solid background information for countering and altering the views of comics-wary administrators, colleagues, or parents.

Some teachers may find they get more from the book by reading it with a colleague. A reading buddy can increase dialogue and critical reflection related to the book's key ideas. And since the buddies are diving into comics together, they can share the workload, reducing the time spent on activity planning and material scrounging. Equally important, reading buddies offer one another emotional support and encouragement—essential items for any teacher exploring nontraditional materials in tradition-bound settings.

That's plenty of prologue. Let's pull on our tights, adjust our capes, and go graphic! Happy flying in Comics Land. I wish everyone a fun and profitable read.

Theory and Research

Theory

A Comic Misunderstanding

About a year before taking keyboard in hand to begin this book, I was doing a second language literacy workshop for middle school teachers in the San Francisco Bay Area. In passing, I mentioned I was researching comics and second language development and that I was considering writing a book on the topic. No one followed up on the remark, so I dropped it, and moved on to several integrated English Language Development (ELD) science and math activities.

But the comment about comics had sparked interest in at least one teacher. After the workshop, a woman in her mid-forties with hair as red as Little Orphan Annie's hurried up to me, shook my hand, thanked me for the inservice, then implored, "You've got to do that book on comics!" She thought comics would excite a lot of her students, add spice to the program, create a low-anxiety environment with all the humor, spur conversation and writing, and generally accelerate second language development. I agreed and lit up; here was a kindred spirit. I bet she had boxes of Patsy Walker and Betty and

Veronica comics in her attic, and a Will Eisner graphic novel sitting on her nightstand.

It took both of us another minute or so to realize that I was talking Spider-Man and Get Fuzzy, and she was talking Buster Keaton, Whoopi Goldberg, and Robin Williams. We had a good chuckle over the misunderstanding and she kindly assured me that she thought my comics would work just as well as her comics with second language learners. Beyond the chuckle, however, the fact that a teacher would hear the word "comics" and immediately think of the stand-up rather than the sit-down-and-read variety underscores the materials' tenuous position in the schools: most teachers have never considered using comics with their second language learners.

Given the infrequent use of comics in second—and first—language programs, you may well be a comics "newbie." If so, a basic definition of comics is a logical starting point. Exactly what kind of material are we talking about here?

Defining Comics

Will Eisner, the legendary comics artist and father of the graphic novel, defines comics simply as "sequential art" (Eisner 1985). *The World Encyclopedia of Comics* offers a slightly expanded definition: "A narrative form containing text and pictures arranged in sequential order (usually chronological)" (Horn 1999, 852). Comics is an umbrella term, and any short, workable definition will miss one or more items under the umbrella. Eisner's definition misses cartoons, single-panel comic art that stands alone without the benefit—or need—of sequence. Horn's definition leaves out expository comics like Gonick and Huffman's The Cartoon Guide to Physics and wordless comics like Aragonés' Actions Speak. But Eisner's and Horn's definitions hold for most comics; most tell a story with words and drawings and have an identifiable beginning, middle, and end.

This book considers the four major types of material under the comics umbrella: cartoons, comic strips, comic books, and graphic novels. All use a style of artwork called cartooning to tell their stories, but each type does the telling with a different format.

CARTOONS offer a slice of life, almost always humorous, in a single, stand-alone panel. The panel (or frame) is the basic building block of all comics. Cartoon captions work in tandem with the drawing to "make the joke." Examples: Bizarro, Marmaduke, and The Far Side.

COMIC STRIPS tell their stories in sequenced, horizontally arranged blocks of usually three to five panels. They're published in thousands of newspapers around the world, the dailies in black and white, the Sunday strips in glorious color. Most of us have these with our breakfast cereal and couldn't face the day without them. Examples: Get Fuzzy, The Fusco Brothers, and Luann.

COMIC BOOKS take the strip format and stretch it to twenty to forty pages. These comics look more like magazines than books, but they've been called books since at least the 1930s and so books they are. Some titles contain complete, one-shot stories, many others feature "continuity plots" that unfold—and typically cliff-hang—issue to issue. Examples: Superman, Donald Duck, and Bone.

GRAPHIC NOVELS are comic books' plumper cousins. In size and scope, they're full-fledged, full-length books, many containing the entire run of stories previously serialized across several comic book issues. Examples: *Ghostworld; Love and Rockets: Poison River;* and *Castle Waiting: The Lucky Road.*

Theoretical Framework

Now that we've defined comics and sketched out the genre's major types, we're ready to tackle the big question: Why use them? With the tons of other good instructional material available, why comics? The rationale for using comics rests on principles pulled from three areas: second language acquisition, brain-based teaching, and progressive literacy.

Second Language Acquisition

If you've got a tie-dyed T-shirt in the bottom of your dresser and a pair of old bell-bottoms hanging in the back of your closet, you're old enough to remember the days of English as a Second Language (ESL) teaching where dialogue memorization, pattern drills, overcorrection, and endless grammar explanations reigned supreme. Over the past couple of decades, countless second language teachers have retooled, switching from grammar-based to communication-based programs, from a focus on form to a focus on message. That revolutionary switch to communicative language teaching (CLT) was driven, in large part, by the work of theorist and researcher Stephen Krashen (1982, 1985, 1992).

Today, Krashen's (2003) notions about the dynamics and optimal conditions for second language development continue to influence how huge numbers of ESL and foreign language teachers do their job. Two cornerstones of Krashen's theory are the input hypothesis (also called the comprehension hypothesis) and the affective filter hypothesis. The input hypothesis claims that we acquire a second language by receiving comprehensible input (understandable messages) and that students get this type of input when they're involved in activities using language for genuine communication. Communication-based activities, as opposed to grammar-based activities where L2 (second language) structures are analyzed and practiced, automatically provide students with language a little beyond their current level, "i," in Krashen's term, and help them move from "i" to the next level up, "i +1." Krashen holds that second language learners acquire L2 structures not by focusing on the form of the message, but on the message itself. The hypothesis further asserts that messages are made more understandable "by utilizing context, extra-linguistic information, and our knowledge of the world" (Krashen 1994, p. 54).

The affective filter hypothesis points to the impact of emotions on second language acquisition. Students who are self-confident and highly motivated tend to make more progress in second language than students who are low in self-esteem and motivation (Gardner and Lambert 1972; Krashen 1982). Moreover, a student's level of anxiety, or "affective filter," plays a big part in determining the amount and speed of second language development. When learners feel worried and on the spot, the affective filter is high and messages have difficulty getting through the filter and "into" the student, regardless of how comprehensible those messages may be. Conversely, learners who are comfortable and secure have a lower affective filter. More understandable messages are available for processing, resulting in greater and faster language acquisition.

Input and affective filter hypotheses are inextricably linked and underpin Krashen's bold, unblushing, and oft-repeated contention that "comprehensible input is the only causative variable in second language acquisition." He maintains that students will acquire a second language "when they obtain comprehensible input and when their affective filters are low enough to allow the input in" (Krashen 1994, 58).

Comics provide both the needed input and positive affect. Abundant visual clues increase the amount of comprehensible input and consequently boost reading comprehension and L2 acquisition. Increased comprehension, in turn, keeps the affective filter low by eliminating or considerably reducing the anxiety and frustration many students feel when confronting "inconsiderate" text, text that is miles above their current independent reading level. Another big reason students may have lower affective filters while doing comics activities is because of the inherent entertainment value of comics—the "fun factor."

> **Field Sketch: Comics and a Low-Anxiety Environment**
>
> Students all like comics. I have used comics several times in my class, and my students did have a very good time. After class they told me they had never felt so relaxed in an English class.
>
> —Xu Yuling, ESL Teacher
> Haicang Experimental Middle School
> Xiamen, China
>
> ■
>
> After reading the graphic novel *Dear Julia:* I think this book is good. I can learn some perfect sentences from this book, vocabulary and grammar. And I'm relax when I read this book. I think it can learn or improve my English to use comics. [unedited comments]
>
> —Zhou Li, Student
> Chuck Kaspar, Instructor
> Intermediate/Adv. ESL Adult Education Class
> Independence Adult Center
> San Jose, California

Social Interaction

Having students read material they comprehend, like, and feel successful with is a key part of any good second language program. But if we want our students to become communicatively competent in their second language, to use language effectively in a variety of settings and for a variety of purposes, they obviously need to do more than read.

Consistent with Vygotsky's (1978) view of the social origins of language and learning, a number of authors (Hatch 1992; McGroarty 1993; Johnson 1995; Celce-Murcia and Olshtain 2000) stress the importance of interaction in learning a second language. Theorist Michael Long's (1983) interaction hypothesis contends that L2 speakers gain comprehensible input as they negotiate meaning and make adjustments during the give and take of conversation. Merrill Swain's (1985) comprehensible output hypothesis claims that second language learners need tasks and activities that require them to speak as much as listen, where they must linguistically stretch and produce Krashen's i +1, not simply hear it. Comprehensible input causes students to focus more on semantics—on meaning. Comprehensible output, Swain believes, causes students to also focus on syntax—how sentences are put together. Good communication clearly depends on an attention to both meaning and syntax, input and output. Taken together, Long and Swain complement Krashen's focus on input by reminding us of the equally significant role that interaction and output play in second language acquisition.

As students interact, either with the teacher or in pairs or small groups, they use language for real communication, asking questions and making statements about the topic at hand. They use all the contextual clues available in face-to-face conversation (a hand gesture, an object, a visual, a request to paraphrase) to make what they say and what they hear more comprehensible.

In heterogeneous groups, native speakers and more advanced second language learners typically serve as "language stretchers" for less proficient students. The stretchers naturally provide lots of Krashen's i +1, language containing some vocabulary and structures a notch or so above their classmates' present level. In collaborative settings, beginning through advanced second language learners actively negotiate meaning, making sense of the world through L2, learning language while using language to learn. Collaborative work also helps students build pragmatic competence. As they interact with native English speakers, nonnative speakers learn the culturally acceptable—and unacceptable—ways of using their new language.

Finally, student-to-student interactions provide time for making friends across cultures. Such friendships take the second-language- and second-culture-learning opportunites in the classroom and extend them to the playground, cafeteria, and neighborhood.

The traditional view of comics sees students either reading or creating comics alone, whether in or outside school, mostly outside. In contrast, nearly all the activities in this book feature student collaboration, and place comics squarely in the classroom. Though activities may have an individual learning component, with students reading, drawing, or writing on their own, most require some interaction in pairs or small groups. At some point, and often at several points in an activity, students exchange ideas and opinions, edit each other's work,

FIG. 1–1 *From* The Shortcut *by Jane d'Rancor. Copyright © 2002 by Jane d'Rancor. Reprinted by permission of Reddingk, <www.reddingk.com/>.*

or collaborate—and negotiate—in teams regarding the fundamental elements of original comics production and publishing.

Authentic Materials

Though communicative language teaching customarily uses some traditional pedagogic materials—commercial materials designed expressly for second language learners—authentic materials form a substantial part of any CLT program, especially those programs with large numbers of intermediate and advanced learners. Authentic materials are any spoken, visual, or written texts used by native speakers; for example, phone calls, email, letters, travel brochures, newspapers, magazines, video game manuals, radio shows, films—and comics. These materials capture the pronunciation, tempo, rhythm, word choices, disfluencies, and informal and formal conventions of everyday speech and writing—how language sounds and what language looks like in the real world of native-level communication.

Comics provide authentic language-learning opportunities for all students, regardless of a learner's second language proficiency level. The dramatically reduced text (see Figure 1–1) of many comics and, for example, make them manageable and language-profitable for even beginning level readers.

TESL Approaches

Three leading TESL (Teaching English as a Second Language) approaches incorporate the above elements: content-based ELD (English Language Development), SDAIE (Specially Designed Academic Instruction in English), and CALLA (Cognitive Academic Language Learning Approach).

Content-based ELD develops second language through activities in science, math, social studies, literature, and the arts, and highlights the key vocabulary and foundation concepts of each curricular area. Though activities always feature some academic content, the primary objective of the approach is to build English language skills, helping students become functionally competent in their new language as quickly as possible. Content-based ELD programs are found at the K–5 level and typically serve students with beginning and early intermediate levels of English language proficiency.

In contrast, the primary objective of SDAIE is to help second language students learn grade-level core curriculum—the same curriculum offered to their native English-speaking peers. English skills are honed and expanded as a natural by-product of content-focused activities. SDAIE, in previous incarnations called Sheltered English Instruction or simply Sheltered Instruction, was originally designed for homogeneously grouped secondary students at the intermediate to early advanced levels (Krashen 1985; Schifini 1988). Today, middle and high schools with large numbers of second language learners continue to offer subjects delivered with an SDAIE approach (SDAIE Algebra or SDAIE American History, for example). The classes, however, compared to a decade or more ago, often contain students with a much wider range of English proficiency stages, including the occasional beginning-level English speaker. SDAIE instruction is characterized by a heavy use of artifacts, models, visuals, videos, graphic organizers, role-plays, collaborative learning, and alternatives to traditional paper-and-pencil assessment (projects, portfolios, and performance-based testing).

CALLA (Chamot and O'Malley 1994) is similar to SDAIE, with a focus on grade-appropriate content and academic language development. In addition to using classic SDAIE strategies, the approach features explicit instruction and practice in a variety of metacognitive, cognitive, and social-affective learning strategies. For example, in reading a social studies text chapter, tenth-grade L2 students might learn to skim for key ideas, elaborate prior knowledge about those ideas, sequence historical events via a storyboard, and work with a reading buddy to make better sense of the text.

Comics obviously offer an element common to all three approaches: visual support. Not so obviously, comics can help with the approaches' focus on content. For example, comics like Gonick's The Cartoon Guide to Statistics, Dignifying Science (see Figure 1–2), Delgado's Age of Reptiles, Lalo Alcaraz's editorial cartoons, and Trudeau's Doonesbury strip, provide comprehensible reading for learning concepts in math, science, and social studies. Finally, comics are useful for teaching learning strategies in CALLA. Wordless or text-light comics, for example, allow students to practice making inferences from context clues—visual or mostly visual clues in this case—without having to struggle with L2 text at the same time.

Brain-Based Teaching

Brain-based teaching is the second area supporting our use of comics with second language learners. Since the 1980s, and often in tandem with the move to communicative language teaching, thousands of educators have modified their instruction to make it more brain-based, teaching in ways that are consistent with how the brain learns best. We now know more about the brain than ever before. Brain-imaging technologies like PET (Positron Emission Tomography), fMRI (Functional Magnetic Resonance Imaging), and EEG (electroencephalography) have allowed neuroscientists to investigate the complex relationships between brain structure and function. Many of the findings offer a window on the learning process, including how we process language.

Several authors (Hart 1983; Sylwester 1995; Caine and Caine 1997; Wolfe 2001) have mined the mountains of brain research for possible applications to the classroom. The result is a set of brain-based practices teachers can use to enhance student learning. Compared to traditional classrooms, brain-compatible classrooms feature more hands-on, manipulative-based activities, simulations, role-plays,

FIG. 1–2 *"Rosalind Franklin" from* Dignifying Science: Stories About Women Scientists *by Jim Ottaviani and Stephanie Gladden. Copyright © 1999 by Jim Ottaviani and Stephanie Gladden. Reprinted by permission of G.T. Labs, <www.gt-labs.com/>.*

projects, and small-group work. Experiential, learn-by-doing methodology replaces the old "sit-and-get." Students are active learners, not passive recipients of knowledge, so teachers talk less and students talk more. More student-to-student interaction means greater opportunities to use—and therefore develop—second language, as students research, experiment, build, problem solve, trade ideas and opinions, and present their new learnings and creations. Two brain-based practices warrant special mention in relation to comics: an emphasis on engaging content and an expanded use of visual material.

Engaging Content

The brain has little time for nonsense. It's a meaning maker, constantly searching for patterns, connecting bits of new information to old, fashioning wholes from parts and parts from wholes. It's also shamelessly self-centered. The brain makes sense of the world in terms of personal learner needs. Relevant curriculum attracts and engages it. Imposed, nonrelevant curriculum leaves it and its third- or tenth-grade owner yawning or staring out the window.

For a number of reasons—the humor, heroes, movement, pop culture themes (see Figure 1–3), real-world language, novelty, and, perhaps above all, artwork—comics consistently engage students. If you ask students at various grade levels why they like comics, one word keeps popping up over and over again: fun. It's a word that makes for brain engagement and a word I wish I heard more often in the schools when we talk about academic curriculum.

Sylwester (1995) reminds us that emotion drives attention and attention drives learning. The more emotionally connected students feel to a piece of material, the more concepts and skills learned. How emotionally connected do students get to comics? I frequently begin a comic strip activity by fishing out a newspaper from my backpack and opening it to the comics section. I hold up the paper and announce that we're going to be doing an activity with "this stuff." Primary students typically squeal with delight and applaud. Older students bob their heads and give me a big "Yeah!," the upper-grade equivalent to the munchkins' yips and claps. I'm sure part of the reaction comes from the sheer freshness of the material since comics are still rare birds in the schools. But seeing that enthusiasm and attention maintained through several comics activities spread over a number of days

FIG. 1–3 *"One Night at Saratoga School"* by Michael Allen and John Orloff originally published in Garish Zow Comics *(no. 5). Copyright © 2004 by Michael Allen and John Orloff. Reprinted by permission of Hidden Agenda Press,* <www.hiddenagendapress.com/>.

or weeks tells me that it's largely the material itself that accounts for the positive, let's-go-to-it! attitude in students.

Students find comics inherently interesting and emotionally invest in them. In fact, many of our students, both first and second language learners, have been investing in comics—out of school—for years. Teachers are often surprised to learn after doing their first comics activity how much students know about particular comics: the names and traits of characters, the nature of the human and animal relationships, the conflicts, the basic story lines, and the running gags. Some students have followed a favorite cartoon, comic strip, or comic book for years. Very few, however, have ever been able to do something with comics in school and hence, have them validated by the teacher as legitimate reading material. When teachers use comics, the material automatically gets the seal of approval. The upshot in brain-based teaching terms: Relevant and engaging out-of-school material is now relevant and engaging in-school material. Emotional buy-in is strong, students attend to the activities, and second language learning accelerates.

> **Field Sketch: Why I Read Comics**
>
> These [comics] are really good, I like it. I have never seen books so interesting like these. [unedited comment]
>
> —Yamileth Menjivar, Freshman
> Elsie Allen High School
> Santa Rosa, California

More Visuals

You only have to work a short time with beginning-level second language students to understand the importance of the second brain-based practice, an expanded use of visuals. Here's a good example: A new teacher I coached a few months ago lovingly referred to her fourth-grade multilingual class as "my quilt." With thirty kids and seven different primary languages, the metaphor was apt. Her students posessed a rich mix of interests, talents, and skills. All the multiple intelligences (Gardner 1983; Armstrong 2000, 2003) were there as they are in nearly every class, in endless combination. Some kids shined in linguistic, logical-mathematical, or visual-spatial endeavors, some more in bodily-kinesthetic, musical, interpersonal, or intrapersonal realms. Other students demonstrated aspects of Gardner's newer naturalist and existential intelligences. But regardless of a student's particular gift or gifts, regardless of favored learning modality, the fourth-grade teacher with the lovely quilt knew that all her beginning to early intermediate second language learners were—by default—visual learners.

All her kids, native speakers included, benefited when she used visual materials. But the square-one and -two English learners, with low oral skills and even lower or nonexistent English literacy skills, were lost without them. How soon into her new teaching career had she learned she needed lots and lots of visuals? About two minutes into the first activity on the first day of school she told me. As she put it, "Without pictures, my beginning English speakers were dead in the water." I've heard the same basic sentiment from dozens and dozens of teachers through the years.

Visuals and Levels of Learning

As we learn, the brain builds neural networks, connecting and organizing information in handy categories. One way to describe that building process is in terms of three levels of learning: concrete, representational (or symbolic), and abstract (Wolfe 2001). It's hard to beat concrete experience for strong and lasting learning. After almost forty-five years, I can still recall with absolute clarity my first ocean swim in Florida. I close my eyes and feel the sand between my toes and the warm water against my face, see the dark blue-green of the Atlantic stretching to the horizon, hear the gulls squawking, smell the suntan lotion on my skin, and taste the salt in the water. All the senses were activated, something we like to do for students in school whenever we can, but how do you bring a whole ocean into the classroom? Or the whole classroom to the ocean if you're in Kansas City?

A second level of learning, the representational or symbolic, is a common—and effective—alternative for students whose teachers lack a museum-sized stockroom of objects or an unlimited field-trip budget. Visual materials—photos, maps, charts, paintings, stick-figure drawings, and professionally done comics—serve as "stand-ins" when the real items are unavailable. A picture with the oral or written label *seagull* is unlikely to carry the learning impact of the flapping, raucous, food-begging real bird, but will have far more impact for learners new to the *seagull* term or concept than the word alone.

The third level of learning presents concepts in the abstract, words with more words, words without concrete or visual representations. School and job success depends in large measure on a person's literacy skills, on the ability to learn and function with abstract language.

How difficult is abstract learning in a second language? Let's take the Spanish word *trompo* as an example. If you're not sure what a *trompo* is, you'll need a definition. Here you go:

> Un trompo es un objeto de forma cónica, hecho de madera. Es un tipo de juguete para niños. El niño lo envuelve con una cuerda y cuando lo tira, hace giros en la tierra.

Now try adding the concept to one of your neural networks, to *juguetes* or perhaps *objetos que hacen giros.* Anyone having trouble plugging in the new word? Readers literate in Spanish hooked *trompo* (top) to *juguetes* (toys) and to *objetos que hacen giros* (objects that spin) long ago, probably around age six or seven. Readers new to Spanish or new to the Spanish word for *top* and many of the words used to define it hit a conceptual brick wall. Without more context—an object, movement, or visual clue—learning a new concept or even a new label for an old concept can be a daunting task for second language learners.

Besides making oral and written text more concrete, and hence more understandable, visuals can increase the number of concepts learned and the length of time those concepts are remembered. All our senses help us learn, of course, and wise teachers have been building concepts and skills in a multimodal format for years, giving students something to see, hear, touch, and even smell and taste, whenever they can. Making sure our activities contain a visual component, however, seems especially important given the vast amounts of information we get by looking; about 70 percent of the body's sensory receptors are found in the eyes (Wolfe 2001).

In second language education, teachers and students know the truth of the old saying that a picture is worth a thousand words. In fact, for beginning and early intermediate students, the right picture at the right time may be worth several times that many words.

> **Field Sketch: Why I Read Comics**
>
> They [comics] are funny and I like because I can understand It have many pictures. [unedited comment]
>
> —David Benitez, Freshman
> Elsie Allen High School
> Santa Rosa, California
>
> ■
>
> I like comic books because they are interesting, funny, easy to read, short, and they have pictures to help you understand. [unedited comment]
>
> —Fernando Garcia, Freshman
> Elsie Allen High School
> Santa Rosa, California

Progressive Literacy

The final part of the theoretical framework borrows three tenets from progressive literacy: engagement through authentic literature, using language for real communication purposes, and a focus on content over form. First, progressive literacy theory maintains that authentic literature—books and stories that are whole rather than excerpted, use rich, natural language, and are personally meaningful—are much more likely to engage students (Goodman 1986; Graves 2002; Goodman in Flurkey and Xu 2003; Smith 1997, 2003). Engaged students are more likely than nonengaged students to want to listen to, read, talk, and write about the content of the literature, whether oral or written. Comics contain whole stories (sometimes via serialized issues) told with natural language, avoiding the stilted, artificial language of controlled vocabulary stories.

Second, progressive literacy theory contends that students improve their language skills by using language for real, learner-centered communication purposes. Progressive-based teachers favor story discussion over story questioning, voluntary reading over mandated reading, and writing for a wide audience over writing only for the teacher.

Consistent with progressive practices, the activities suggested in Chapter 3 emphasize teacher-facilitated "grand conversations." Students react to and freely discuss interesting aspects of the comics they read, a far cry from the teacher question-grilling that dominates traditional story "discussion" (Where did the story take place? Who was the main character? What happened first in the story?). Moreover, the activities give students a huge choice in what they read, rather than having titles dictated by the teacher, reading program publisher, or a district or state curriculum committee. Finally, students write for a variety of authentic purposes and audiences. There are no forced-writing story starters, as in: If I had the superpowers of Daredevil I would . . . or One way I'm like the character GoGirl! is . . . Students respond to favorite comics with journal entries and book reports. They also write for the teacher, classmates, friends, family, local community, and online readers as they create a variety of original comics.

The third tenet from progressive literacy places the instructional focus on content, echoing a key principle we saw earlier in SDAIE and CALLA. Edelsky, Altwerger, and Flores (1991, 23) remind us that ". . . learning language happens in the course of attending to and learning something else . . ." Comics build L2 skills across all language subsystems—phonology, morphology, syntax, lexicon, semantics, and pragmatics—as students attend to the many "something elses" residing within the material: content, the full gamut of life's facts and fancies, adventures and mishaps, terrors and temptations, joys and sorrows. Language form (or accuracy) is addressed—and addressed directly with minilessons, for example, on affixes, adjective-noun order, verb form shifts, colloquialisms, or the use of quotation marks—but always in the service of content learning.

A Look at the Research

We've built the theoretical framework from good timber: principles derived from second language acquisition, brain-based teaching, and progressive literacy. Using comics for second language development makes great sense—theoretically. These nontraditional materials should work, but do they? Do comics help students develop second language skills? Can they help with content learning? New culture learning? Do they work with both children and adults? Can they be used with students at any language proficiency stage—square-one beginners through advanced learners? What does the research say regarding these and other questions related to comics in the multilingual classroom?

Literature abounds on second language acquisition (SLA) methodology. Type in "second language instruction," or "ESL" as search terms at the Ask ERIC (Educational Resources Information Center) website and you'll find thousands of journal articles, books, guides, reports, and conference papers. The professional literature on comics is also substantial. Rhode and Bullough's (2003) Comics Research Bibliography contains nearly 17,000 entries covering a dizzying range of subjects, everything from Mexican comic books, French graphic novels, and the history of Superman, to censorship, stereotypes, sexism, wordless comics, and comic strip journalism.

There are relatively few studies and articles, however, that look specifically at the intersection of the two areas: using comics as a vehicle for second language acquisition. Given that dearth of research, the review that follows includes studies and articles targeting comics and second language learners and others that target comics and native English speakers. Findings from native speaker studies are discussed in terms of their potential application to nonnative speakers. Generalizing from first to second language students is warranted given the many similarities between first and second language development

(Dulay, Burt, and Krashen 1982; Brown 2000). As we generalize, however, it's important to remember that L1 and L2 development is similar, but not identical. Second language learners are "language wise," having already acquired many of the key elements of their first language. Moreover, all second language learners, but especially older learners, have significant amounts of subject matter knowledge learned through the first language. Both stockpiles of knowledge—language and content—help make L2 materials and activities more understandable, and hence, facilitate L2 acquisition.

Organization

The literature review is organized into two parts. Part 1 contains studies and articles focusing on the use of commercial comics. Part 2 contains those focusing on the use of student-made comics. This arrangement by material type helps teachers match comic to learning outcome. Some outcomes require titles from your local comics shop; others call for comics drawn and written by students. Still others, for example, learning about World War II and improving narrative writing skills, may call for both. Regardless of where a study or article is pigeonholed, however, the common denominator is the use of comics to develop academically successful second language learners.

Part One: Commercial Comics

Major topics addressed in this section include comics and

- pleasure reading
- bridge reading
- reading achievement
- teacher, staff, and parent attitudes
- humor
- student reading preferences
- school-authorized reading
- text ownership
- aspects of spoken discourse

Swain (1978) administered a questionnaire about comic book and comic strip reading to 169 students in grades 4 through 12 in Durham, North Carolina. Students were divided into two groups, about half making "good" grades (a grade point average, or GPA, of 3.0 or higher), the other half making "poor" grades (a GPA of 1.0 or below). Huge numbers of students in all grades reporting reading comics. For example, 100 percent of the "good"-grade and 89 percent of the "poor"-grade elementary students read comic books and/or comic strips. By the high school years, the percentages were only slightly different, with 95 percent of the "good"-grade and 90 percent of the "poor"-grade students reading one or both types of material. Throughout the grades, the "good"-grade students read more comics than the "poor"-grade students. Students who read comics also read other types of books. A little over 90 percent of the "good"-grade students and almost 80 percent of the "poor"-grade students reported reading library books.

Many students also reported that besides helping them become better readers and spellers, comics had helped them learn more content, for example, more about astronomy, animals, famous people, history, and geography. Swain concludes that comics may be effective in reading and language arts classes because of their popularity, aid to content learning, and the fact that they don't discourage students from reading other materials.

Ujiie and Krashen (1996) confirm Swain's (1978) findings about the popularity of comics. The researchers surveyed 571 seventh graders at two schools in Southern California regarding comic book reading. One school was middle class; the other was a Chapter 1 school where a little over 80 percent of the students qualified for free or reduced-price lunch. Twenty-eight percent of the students at the Chapter 1 school were classified as LEP (Limited English Proficient).

There was no significant difference between schools in how often students read comics. Analysis of the results, however, was restricted to boys, since boys read comics far more than girls in both samples. Around half the girls in the survey said they never read comics. Eighty-three percent of the boys at the middle-class school reported they always or sometimes read comics; at the Chapter 1 school, the figure was nearly identical at 82 percent.

On attitudes about reading, a little over half of the heavy and occasional comic book readers at the middle-class school told researchers they liked to read. Only 21 percent of the noncomic book readers liked to read. At the Chapter 1 school, a third of the comic book readers liked to read compared with only 4 percent of non–comic book readers. When students were asked if they read books (other than comic books), 70 percent of the comics readers at the middle-class school said yes versus 46 percent of the non–comics readers. At the Chapter 1 school, a little over half of the comics readers said they read books compared to a little under a third of the non–comics readers.

Findings from the study help demolish one of the enduring myths about comics reading, that comics somehow inhibit an interest in other types of reading. Quite the contrary: at both schools, boys who read more comics also read more for pleasure, enjoyed reading more, and read more books (other than comics). The authors speculate that since frequency of reading and reading ability are consistently related in reading studies, comic book readers may well be better readers.

Finally, Ujiie and Krashen were surpised by the fact that despite the high cost of comics, middle-class and far less affluent students read comics at the same frequency. The authors conclude that the Chapter 1 students either have a cheaper source for comics (friends? the library?) or are spending limited funds on comics. Both possibilities, but especially the latter, argue for the "attractiveness of comics" as reading material.

Support for Ujiie and Krashen's (1996) "more reading equals better reader" hypothesis comes from Anderson, Wilson, and Fielding (1988), who looked at the relation between amount of reading and reading achievement in 155 fifth graders. For eight to twenty-six weeks, students kept track of the total minutes per day devoted to out-of-school reading. Reading categories included books, comics, mail, and newspapers and magazines. The findings will come as no surprise to veteran teachers, who have noted the reading habits of their students for years: most children do little out-of-school reading; those who do read, however, are more proficient readers. Specifically, the researchers found that the amount of book reading students do is the best predictor of reading achievement. Moreover, there was a small but significant positive relationship between amount of book reading and comic book reading. Students who read more books also read more comic books. In a statement that should put a smile on the face of literature-based reading teachers everywhere, the authors declare that, "The case can be made that reading books is a cause, not merely a reflection, of reading proficiency" (302).

Like Ujiie and Krashen (1996), Russikoff and Pilgreen (1994) found that comics, far from locking students into a lifetime of light reading, actually served as a conduit to heavier, more complex reading. The authors surveyed eighteen doctoral students at a Southern California university regarding reading patterns and preferences as youth and adults. Eighty-two percent of the students indicated that they enjoyed light reading when young. Light reading, as defined by the researchers, included comic books, magazines, newspapers, and a variety of novels (mystery, science fiction, sports, adventure, romance). How often did these students "go light"? Nearly 95 percent reported reading light materials daily or several times a week as kids.

Responses on the open-ended questionnaire showed that the number one choice in light reading was comic books, followed by magazines, then romance, mystery, and adventure novels. Almost all students stated that they continued to enjoy a variety of light reading today. But, obviously, as adult doctoral students, all had gone on to more advanced and more challenging reading—textbooks, professional journals, and instructional manuals.

The study supports the hypothesis that light reading leads to more serious reading and should help calm the fears of those teachers and parents who still believe that "going light," especially with comics, means "staying light." One caveat related to terminology. Comics fans typically bristle when all comics are labeled "light." Many comics are lightweight fare, but many others are demanding—and serious—reads. In one of my recent workshops, a middle school teacher paged through *Barefoot Gen: A Cartoon Story of Hiroshima* and *The Last Lonely Saturday*, a mostly wordless graphic novel about a grieving widower, then turned to me and declared, "Heavy stuff!" Exactly.

Finally, a reading preference study by Worthy, Moorman, and Turner (1999) offers additional evidence regarding the popularity of comics among middle school students. It also examines student preferences in relation to the availability of favorite materials at school. In a survey of 419 sixth-grade students at three schools in a socioeconomically and ethnically diverse district in Texas, researchers found that the two most preferred types of reading material were scary books (like R. L. Stine's Goosebumps series) at 66 percent and cartoons and comics at 65 percent. Popular magazines were a distant third at 38 percent. Comics, in fact, placed in the top two or three preferred materials regardless of students' income, reading achievement, attitude toward reading, or—contrary to Ujiie and Krashen (1996)—gender. Among girls, comics ranked third in popularity, after scary books and magazines.

Researchers also interviewed teachers and librarians regarding their opinions on using student-preferred materials. Finally, to check on the availability of the preferred items, the authors visited each class and library and inventoried materials. Perhaps the most interesting— and troubling—aspect of the findings is the disconnect between what students liked to read and what schools provided. Out of the top ten favorites, the only material that earned a "very good" label for availability was ninth-ranked funny novels. Scary books, students' number one preference, had only "moderate" availability, with sports (fourth) and drawing books (fifth) rated "limited." Access to popular magazines, third on the list, was "very limited." As to the second most preferred material, cartoons and comics, cartoon books were available in only one library and one classroom. Comic books were "unavailable," meaning absent from all three libraries and all twelve classrooms.

Staff attitudes help explain the unavailability of comics. Two of the three librarians surveyed felt that comic books were inappropriate for school, though none disapproved of comic strip books like Garfield. Many of the teachers, too, saw comics as unsuitable, something to read at home perhaps, but not at school.

Anti-comics sentiments like these, which I occasionally hear from teachers when I suggest the use of comics, harken back to Wertham (1954). In *Seduction of the Innocent: The Influence of Comic Books on Today's Youth*, and in testimony before the U.S. Senate Subcommittee Investigating Juvenile Delinquency in 1954 (Horn 1999), psychiatrist Fredric Wertham claimed that comic books contributed to a variety of social ills, including illiteracy. Unfortunately, despite ample evidence to the contrary here (and see additional reviews in Krashen 1993; and Dorrell, Curtis, and Rampal 1995), some educators still believe that comics retard rather than aid language development.

Dorrell and Carroll (1981) offer a powerful counterexample to the anti-comics stance of librarians and teachers in the Texas district found in Worthy, Moorman, and Turner (1999). In an underused middle school library in Columbia, Missouri, the researchers gathered student traffic and material circulation data over two time periods. During the control period of fifty-seven days, only standard (non-comics) materials were available. During the treatment period of seventy-four days, which immediately followed the control phase, the researchers placed a rack of noncirculating comics in the library. Data analysis showed an increase of 82 percent in library traffic and an increase of 30 percent in the circulation of non-comics materials during the comics treatment period. The authors conclude that the comics served as a catalyst for library usage. Moreover, parent and staff support for comics in the library was strong, especially among the school's reading and special education teachers.

Interested in understanding why comics, and Archie comics in particular, engage so many students, Norton (2003) interviewed thirty-four Archie comics readers (nineteen girls and fifteen boys) at a school in Vancouver, Canada. Thirteen of the grade 5, 6, and 7 students she spoke with were second language learners with home languages of Mandarin, Cantonese, Korean, Swedish, Bengali, and Farsi.

In addition to the interviews, the researcher used student questionnaires to help her answer three specific questions: (1) "Why do children read Archie comics?" (2) "How do readers of Archie comics relate to one another?" and (3) "How is the reading of Archie comics contrasted with school-authorized literacy practices?" The questionnaires included an Archie story so that students would have something specific on which to base their responses.

In answer to question one, Norton found that lots of kids read Archie comics because they find the books funny. Twenty-five students (out of thirty who answered the question) mentioned humor when asked why they liked to read Archie. Beyond the humor, students said the comics were "fun to look at" and found the characters interesting and engaging. Visuals were an important element for second language learners. One L2 learner noted (unedited), "Well, they got picture, can help them, colorful pictures to help the readers to understand like how, what is happening, going on" (p. 143).

As to question two and how Archie readers relate to one another, Norton discovered that students, particularly girls, had developed an "informal and loosely connected reading community." Students in the Archie comics community traded comics, introduced their friends to them, often read comics together, and regularly discussed the stories. My neighborhood friends and I did exactly the same thing some forty-three years ago with our superhero comics.

For question three, dealing with school-authorized literacy practices, Norton reports that teachers and parents largely saw comics as "a waste of time." Reading comics was discouraged. Students had learned that Archie wasn't "educational" or "challenging." Chapter books were fine for silent reading, but not Archie. Students knew that Archie, Betty, Veronica, Jughead, and the whole Riverdale crew was unauthorized reading.

Insights from Archie readers offer two challenges for literacy educators. The first deals with student choice. The author contends that pleasure reading is related to "a sense of ownership of text." This ownership, developed through material self-selection, produced engaged readers, students who read comics "energetically and critically." Unfortunately, despite students' enthusiasm for Archie comics and how much reading, discussion, and comprehensible input for second language learners they generated, Norton reports that ". . . children's reading preferences received little recognition or validation from teachers or parents" (p. 145). Norton urges teachers to look carefully at the type of reading students find pleasurable and meaningful—in and out of the classroom—and to consider how such material including comics might be successfully woven into the curriculum.

The second challenge deals with our vision of literacy. While never discounting the importance of the written word, Norton asks teachers to reconceptualize and broaden our notion of literacy and how we develop it in the classroom. Multimodal texts, including comics, Internet hypertext, and CD-ROMs, allow meaning making via words, graphics, sound, and video—a crucial combination of supports for beginning second language learners often overwhelmed by conventional written text.

Williams (1995) reminds us that second language learners can be just as overwhelmed by spoken discourse. The author advocates the use of comic strips as a means to help students deal with "the ambiguity, vagueness and downright sloppiness of spoken English" (p. 25). Williams worked with low intermediate adults in an intensive ESL program at the American Language Institute at New York University. Students could easily cite chapter and verse on grammar rules and were scoring high on multiple choice grammar tests. Conversation, however, was a different matter; discourse skills were rock bottom. Most students were "unable to string more than three English words together without using a dictionary" (p. 2).

Needing material to improve his students' conversational skills and knowing that mainstream ESL course books typically neglect spoken discourse, Williams turned to *Yukon Ho!*, a collection of Calvin and Hobbes strips by Bill Watterson, as a course book. The strips provided authentic, interactional English and also helped Williams avoid the traditional presentation-practice approach, where the teacher describes a small element of language, provides the rule for its use, and then sets students off to practice it. Specifically, the strips built awareness of a variety of common—and essential—aspects of spoken discourse, including:

- ellipsis ("Nice room" for "What a nice room.")
- blends ("Outta my way!")
- nonwords ("uh-huh," "hmph," "sheesh!")
- vague lexis ("and stuff," "or something")
- confirmation checks ("Pretty scary, huh?")
- contrastive stress ("This is MY room.")
- new topic signals ("How about . . .?" "Do you think . . .?")
- nonverbal language (body language and facial expressions)
- mitigators ("I guess . . .")
- routine/ritual phrases ("It's great to see you, Max!")

Analyzing the Calvin and Hobbes strips in terms of why characters say what they say rather than simply what "X" or "Y" means, gave students the chance to "see English differently." Students not only gained pragmatic knowledge—understandings about the appropriate use of language in different social contexts—but became more active language learners in the process.

Part Two: Student-Made Comics

Major topics addressed in this section include comics and

- language and content assessment
- syntax, mechanics

- insights into the writing process
- content learning (history, politics, social issues)
- literacy, critical thinking skills

In a study with second- and third-grade L2 learners (Cary 1998), storyboards were used to determine comprehension levels of teacher-told stories. A storyboard is a type of comic strip with panels and sketches that sequence a story's major scenes and plot turns. They are frequently used by filmmakers as a planning tool before shooting any film or video footage. In this study, student storyboards combined sequenced drawings and written text. Stories were told using what I called the Contextualized Storytelling Approach (CSA). CSA uses objects, visuals, movement, sound effects, speech modification techniques, and teacher-facilitated story discussion to make the language and content of L2 oral stories comprehensible.

The twelve target students, six boys and six girls, were all of Mexican heritage and ranged in English language proficiency from beginning through intermediate levels. Because students were unfamiliar with storyboarding, each of the three teacher-tellers modeled the basic process on a chalkboard or chart paper, using a read-aloud story as an example and filling storyboard panels with student-suggested drawings and comments.

Teachers told one world folktale per week for four weeks. After hearing and discussing each tale, students worked individually on large six-panel storyboard sheets (Figures 1–4 and 1–5). A boxed-in space below each panel provided room for student writing. Students were asked to retell the story with drawings and text. The writing could be in English, Spanish, or both. Teachers and I served as scribes for some students and recorded student-dictated text. A little over half the storyboards were written in English, with a little under 5 percent written in English and Spanish. Storyboarding sessions lasted from thirty to fifty minutes.

Though the study focused on the effectiveness of contextualized storytelling for increasing the comprehension of L2 oral narrative and the quantity of L2 speaking, student success with storyboarding warrants special mention here. For students with low English literacy, traditional paper-and-pencil assessment has an obvious drawback; students are unable to show the teacher that they understand a concept using English writing. This inability to demonstrate competence can lead to substantial student frustration and the possible loss of self-

FIG. 1–4 *Second grader working on a storyboard, Franklin School, San Jose, California.*

esteem. In this study, regardless of how much English students had to work with, all were able to use storyboarding to show (literally!) their understanding of the stories. Once familiar with the technique, the students could also use it to storyboard news events, biographies, solutions to a school or social problem, a week's worth of weather conditions, or the steps taken in an experiment on magnetism.

Moreover, the storyboards served as much more than simply an alternative assessment tool for measuring comprehension. Students also used the storyboards as "road maps" for orally retelling the stories to teachers, parents, siblings, and friends. Finally, based on their work as scribes (and editors), teachers reported that the storyboarding provided a meaningful context to work on—and improve—students' English syntax and mechanics (spelling, capitalization, and punctuation) (see Figures 1–6, 1–7, and 1–8).

Beyond their role in assessing comprehension and teaching word order and mechanics, student-made comics may offer some important insights into the writing process. Holmes and Moulton (1994)

FIG. I–5 *Author discussing storyboard details with a second grader, Franklin School, San Jose, California.*

used student-made comics to investigate how university ESL students approached the task of writing. Building on Black's (1991) similar work with native English speakers, the researchers asked a class of eighteen advanced composition students to draw cartoons (create a storyboard/comic strip) showing the steps they followed when tackling an academic writing assignment in English. The class was ethnically diverse, with ten cultures represented.

So that students understood the focus was on the personal writing process and not on producing quality artwork, the instructor modeled a few panels using simple stick figures. The finished comics confirmed that only a few students were using any prewriting strategies. Most students, in fact, showed no prewriting strategies at all; for example, brainstorming, considering and rejecting topics, researching at the library, or talking with others to gain additional information about a topic. Alarmingly—from a teacher's viewpoint—only two students

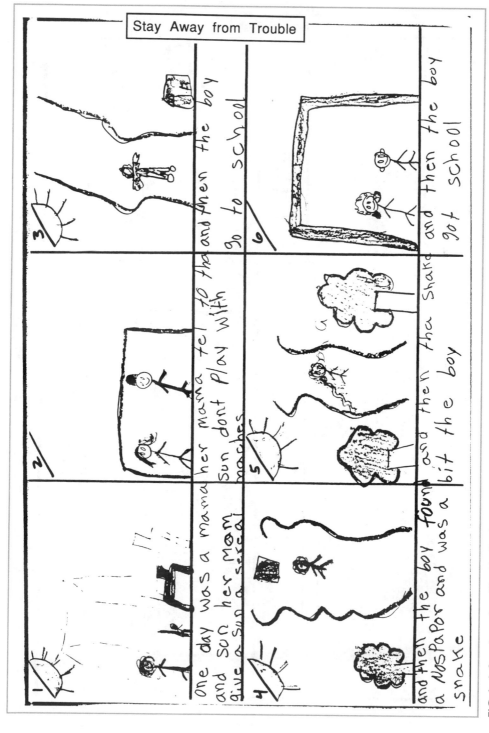

FIG. 1–6. Stay Away from Trouble. Student storyboard, grade 3, Franklin School, San Jose, California.

FIG. I–7 *Lion on the Path. Student storyboard (teacher scribe), grade 2, Franklin School, San Jose, California.*

FIG. 1–8 *The Magic Spoon.* Student storyboard, grade 3, Franklin School, San Jose, California.

depicted themselves organizing ideas before plunging right into the writing. Just as troubling, few demonstrated any sense that their writing might need some revision beyond minor fix-ups for mechanics on the way to a final draft. The comics provided a vehicle for student reflection and helped both students and instructor pinpoint key areas of the writing process needing attention.

Chilcoat (1993) shows how student-generated comics can be used to increase interest in a content area many students find dull and deadly: history. The low interest stems in large part from the predominance of what the author terms verbal-linear activities in the traditional history classroom: lectures, worksheets, and expository writing assignments. Comic book making, with its emphasis on visual representation as a cognitive tool for examining the past and personally interpreting and connecting it to the present, offers an alternative to the typical verbal-linear format. Comic construction increases student interest in history and with it, history learning. The article focuses on the Civil Rights movement and includes sample work from a student-created comic book on Rosa Parks and the Montgomery bus boycott.

Chilcoat and Ligon (1994) offer additional examples of using student-made comics for exploring history, politics, and social issues. Students first investigate historical events like the first deployment of U.S. combat troops to Vietnam in 1965, the My Lai massacre of 1968, the Kent State shootings of 1970, and the Wounded Knee hostage crisis of 1973. Then, using the underground comix genre of the mid-1960s to the mid-1970s as a model, they create historically accurate comic books.

Wright and Sherman (1999) advocate student-made comic strips for building literacy and critical thinking skills at the elementary and middle school levels. They describe an interdisciplinary approach combining language and art where students are involved in all aspects of comic strip production, from idea generating and scripting, to lettering, drawing, and inking. The authors show that a three-panel format can help students learn basic story structure (beginning, middle, and end) as well as the essential elements of setting, character, dialogue, and action.

Morrison, Bryan, and Chilcoat (2002) recommend using pop culture media like comics, film, and music, with middle and high school students—and across all curriculum areas. They acknowledge the reluctance of some teachers to use such media and offer a three-point rationale for their inclusion. One, the media play a significant part in the lives of most students. Their use helps connect students' outside world and pursuits to school. Two, using popular media provides students with opportunities to become critical consumers, better able to judge the quality and accuracy of media content. And three, though this may seem too obvious for words, the researchers underscore the fact that popular media are popular: students enjoy them. Why not play to that popularity and enjoyment?

In particular, the authors advocate student-made comic books because of the activity's capacity for developing language skills and content learning. The time commitment for the activity is considerable, since students must learn the procedures of comic construction as well as the content going into the comic, but educationally justified. Student-made comics integrate language arts, visual arts, and one or more content areas. The authors report that students increase skills in a variety of areas, including researching, expository and historical/biographical writing, dialogue writing, and nonverbal communication. Moreover, they improve reading comprehension strategies while locating main ideas and summarizing and organizing key plot points for their narratives. Finally, class discussions or a school comic book convention allows students to share their creations and demonstrate the extent of their learning. (See "Comics from Scratch" in Chapter 3.)

Two for One

Taken as a whole, the studies and articles reviewed here suggest that comics-based activities are an effective vehicle for second language acquisition and content learning. Our second language learners require high levels of both to succeed in school and the marketplace. Fortunately, the two areas of learning are mutually supportive. Comics activities that help students build L2 oral and literacy skills also make content learning in L2 easier. Conversely, activities that help students learn L2 content also build second language skills.

Questions

Teachers' Questions About Comics

In the last chapter, we answered two fundamental questions about using comics with second language learners: Why use them? and Do they work? In this chapter, we tackle a host of additional questions regarding the ins and outs of comics implementation.

Teachers have questions, of course, with any new instructional material. Comics, however, always generate more than their fair share. And for good reason. Long-standing concerns over the appropriateness and educational value of the materials have made them rare birds in the schools. Consequently, few teachers have ever seen comics "in flight"—enthusiastically read, discussed, written about, and created by students. Moreover, few have ever seen comics-centered activities modeled or even heard comics mentioned in university teacher-prep programs or staff development workshops.

This scarcity of both comics and information on how to use them produces a ton of questions any time I'm in a university class, school, or conference and mention The Fusco Brothers, Baldo, Alison Dare, or a favorite graphic novel in the same breath with second language development. Over the past several years, I've kept track of the many questions teachers pose about comics. The teachers have come from all grade and experience levels and their most frequently asked questions form the basis of the chapter. The questions are organized in five categories:

- curriculum fit
- appropriateness
- variety and availability
- cost and durability
- readability

I've framed the questions as teachers typically ask them and have tried to capture the pragmatic tone and natural give-and-take of a workshop setting. Though some readers may have already jumped ahead to the activities chapter, I'm hoping most of you are still with me right here. Information gleaned in this chapter won't guarantee the success of all comics activities, but should smooth their implementation, help you avoid common pitfalls, and increase the amount of language and content learning for your L2 learners.

Curriculum Fit

How big a part should comics play in my classroom?

As a comics fan and teacher who's seen the learning power of comics across the grades, I'm tempted to answer: A huge part! Understanding, however, that students, teachers, and programs come in all shapes and sizes, with vastly different instructional needs and goals, the answer must be slightly muted: As big a part as you, your students, and the Program Powers That Be deem wise and workable.

Ok, what's generally wise and workable?

Keeping in mind the need for curriculum variety, teachers using comics—or any material for that matter, other than mandated materials – naturally let learning payoff dictate amount of use. The more learning teachers get from comics-based activities, the more you see them using comics. Time devoted to comics varies greatly, from K–5 teachers who do a daily ten- to twenty-minute comic strip activity, to middle school teachers occasionally encouraging comics during SSR (Sustained Silent Reading), to high school and adult ed ESL teachers who may do only one comic book or graphic novel unit in a semester or a year.

Those examples may give the impression that comic usage automatically decreases as we move up the grades. Though often the case, the rule is hardly ironclad. In fact, I've run across enough counterexamples in my consulting practice to know that upper-grade and adult ed teachers are just as likely as lower-grade teachers to use comics, if the teachers have adequate information on their use and, again, are getting plenty of learning mileage from them.

Of course, it's also possible that even with the right information and the potential for lots of learning, comics may simply not be the smartest way to go. A good example is the adult ed teacher I coached a few years ago who was teaching a short-term class of beginning to early intermediate second language learners. These newly arrived immigrants needed basic get-the-job English and we both decided that helping them read the classified ads, use the bus system, and get through a job interview offered more than comics.

So, comics aren't for all teachers in all settings?

Right. I'm not promoting comics as the be-all-end-all material. Granted, I'd love to get more teachers using comics, given the medium's language-building potential and its woeful underutilization in the multilingual classroom. But Ziggy, Zippy, and Batman won't turn a beginner into a near-native speaker in a year. And by themselves, Mutts and Frank & Ernest strips won't build high levels of literacy for all our second language learners. I'm selling comics here, but I'm selling them in moderation, as part of a harmonious mix of materials and activities. Comics work, but they don't work miracles.

Comics can play a significant role in some settings; for example, in elementary classrooms, or in adult ESL American culture and conversation classes. They can play an important, but smaller role in high school ELD (English Language Development) and SDAIE (Specially Designed Academic Instruction in English) classes, and a smaller role still in EOP (English for Occupational Purposes) programs for hotel workers or electronics assemblers. Finally, comics may have only a walk-on part or no part at all in most university EAP (English for Academic Purposes) courses.

Comics, like any material we use for second language development—from ESL readers and Internet news reports to academic writing texts and travel brochures—must help us meet student needs and program goals and objectives. When they do, let's use them; when they don't, let's not. That said, teachers new to the material are usually surprised at how often comics fit the bill—meet those needs, goals, and objectives—and in how many different settings, and with so many different types of students.

Appropriateness

I'm uncomfortable with the sexual, sexist, and violent images in some comics. Why would I sanction their use in the classroom?

You wouldn't. And neither would I, unless I could use those images in a high school or adult learner classroom to critically examine issues of sexuality, sexism, or violence in society. Instructional material needs to work for both students and teacher. Teachers put off by certain comics and not wanting to use the material as grist for the thinking mill can share their concerns with students and suggest—and provide—alternative titles.

But there are some really raunchy comics on the market, right?

Right. Along with raunchy books, magazines, video games, computer games, films, and TV shows. Comics are no different from any of those other media in terms of raunch; raunch comes with the entertainment territory. What teachers new to comics may not realize, however, is that, again, like other media, comics are multifaceted and offer a broad range of content. Raunch is only one small part of a very big comics world.

OK, but even a non-raunchy comic can have an objectionable image or two. Won't a tiny bit of nudity, for example, upset some students and parents?

Guaranteed. I call this the "naked buns" effect. It's the rare student or parent who objects to the *words* "naked buns." But an *image* of naked buns can set off fireworks. Place a comic in the classroom showing somebody's unclothed backside, and suddenly you've got an irate parent calling you at home to complain. The calls will quadruple with an unclothed frontside. Ironically, the "naked buns" effect bolsters the case for comics. The power of images to command attention, to move, to directly communicate, explains, in part, why comics are such a powerful learning medium.

So, bring on the naked buns?

Obviously, we use discretion when choosing materials. We want them grade appropriate and there seems little sense in picking comics we know many students and parents will find offensive when other comics will do the instructional job just as well. But at some point, our use of comics—with or without a naked bun on display—may offend someone. Most teachers are willing to accomodate the offended student or parent by offering alternative material whenever possible. The more serious problem comes from those parents who, in their zeal to protect their own child from what they see as moral, philosophical, or political corruption, demand that the offending comic be pulled from the classroom or library, thereby denying other students access to the material.

The American Library Association's Office for Intellectual Freedom compiles data on challenges to school and public library materials. If you do have a comic challenged, it will be in exceedingly good company. Here's a list of the ALA's top ten most challenged books between 1990 and 2000 (American Library Association 1990–2000).

1. Scary Stories (series) (Alvin Schwartz)
2. *Daddy's Roommate* (Michael Willhoite)
3. *I Know Why the Caged Bird Sings* (Maya Angelou)
4. *The Chocolate War* (Robert Cormier)
5. *The Adventures of Huckleberry Finn* (Mark Twain)
6. *Of Mice and Men* (John Steinbeck)
7. Harry Potter (series) (J. K. Rowling)
8. *Forever* (Judy Blume)
9. *Bridge to Terabithia* (Katherine Paterson)
10. Alice (series) (Phyllis Reynolds Naylor)

What's the best way of handling a challenge?

I'm not sure there is a "best" way, but here's one way that's helped several teachers deal successfully with material challenges. Always listen respectfully to any student or parent objection, explain you had no intention of giving offense, and offer alternative material to the student when possible. Then make it clear—in as diplomatic a manner as you can muster—that under no condition will you purge the comic from the classroom and deny other students the chance to read something you believe has such high educational value.

If for any reason parents aren't satisfied, it's essential that we inform them of their right to appeal and to take their concern to the principal or district office personnel. Most schools and libraries have a formal set of procedures in place for material challenges. If your school is without one, the American Library Association's Office for Intellectual Freedom can help you create a set. Please see Chapter 4 for ALA contact information.

So, expect a challenge if I use comics?

Not at all. Challenges are relatively rare. But it makes good sense to be ready if one arises. Know what to say and know what to do. What is much more likely than a full-blown challenge is a simple query from a parent asking the Why comics? question, comparable to the Why videos? or Why field trips? questions. Most parents aren't anti-comics, but they typically need a little reassuring that comics will have some learning payoff. Older students, and especially adult learners, will need the same reassuring. So we reassure. One way of doing that is to share some of the information from the theory and research chapter. Keeping our students and parents informed of what we're doing and why we're doing it will prevent most problems.

Variety and Availability

Beyond the superhero and humor comics, what's available?

Everything. That answer may surprise you if you skipped comics as a kid and if your current comics reading is limited to a few favorite yuck-yuck strips in the morning newspaper. Superheroes abound, of course, and lots of comics are humorous and remind us why comics are called comics: the first examples from the late nineteenth century were mostly played for laughs. Over the last hundred years or so, however, comics have expanded far beyond the comical. These days, both Batman and Broom Hilda have some pretty stiff competition. Today's comics are published in a broad range of genres, from mystery, horror (see Figure 2–1), fantasy, sci-fi, and romance, to western, war, politics, history, biography, and contemporary fiction (see Figure 2–2).

Chances are, there's at least one type of comic that will catch the interest of most students at any age and grade level. To get a feel for the diversity of offerings, readers may want to thumb through the comics review section in Chapter 4.

I think of comics as fast reads, even those with denser text. What's available for longer, prolonged reading?

Lots. Comics come in all sizes, from single-panel cartoons and the typical three-to-five-panel comic strips, to comic books (usually about thirty pages) and the much larger, book-length graphic novels. One-shot gag cartoons like Strange Brew or In the Bleachers are a quickie read with minimal amounts of text. Graphic novels like Craig Thompson's *Blankets,* Jeff Smith's *Bone* series, Katsuhiro Otomo's six-volume sci-fi adventure *Akira,* or Koike and Kojima's *Lone Wolf and Cub* samurai epic at twenty-eight volumes and over nine thousand pages—delivered direct to your classroom door by forklift truck—provide students with extended reads.

Are girls reading comics as much as boys?

Not yet. Walk into any comics shop or comics convention and you'll see dramatically more males than females thumbing through the bins and standing in line to get a favorite artist's autograph. And the vast majority are young, in their teens to late twenties. Literacy studies and interviews with comics retailers confirm the relatively small number of female comics readers in the United States. In their survey of nearly six hundred seventh graders at two middle schools in Southern California, Ujiie and Krashen (1996) found that boys read comics considerably more often than girls. A little over 80 percent of the boys reported reading comics "always" or "sometimes." Only half the girls read comics at the same frequency. A little over 17 percent of the boys said they "never" read comics versus nearly 50 percent of the girls.

FIG. 2–1a *"Confessions" by Samuel Kienbaum and Jeff Faerber originally published in Garish Zow Comics (no. 5). Copyright © 2004 by Samuel Kienbaum and Jeff Faerber. Reprinted by permission of Hidden Agenda Press,* <www.hiddenagendapress.com/>.

FIG. 2–1b continued. *"Confessions" by Samuel Kienbaum and Jeff Faerber originally published in Garish Zow Comics (no. 5). Copyright © 2004 by Samuel Kienbaum and Jeff Faerber. Reprinted by permission of Hidden Agenda Press,* <www.hiddenagendapress.com/>.

FIG. 2–2 *"This Is"* by Thien Pham originally published in Garish Zow Comics (no. 5). Copyright © 2004 by Thien Pham. Reprinted by permission of Hidden Agenda Press, <www.hiddenagendapress.com/>.

Owner Joe Ferrara of Atlantis Fantasyworld in Santa Cruz, California, reports that only about a quarter of his customers are women ("Better Retailing: Expanding Your Sales to Women" 2001). But many girls and women do read comics, and in ever growing numbers. Joe Field, owner of Flying Colors Comics in Concord, California, reports that the number of his female customers has doubled over the last eight years, moving from 15 percent to the current 30 percent (personal communication 2004). Three factors help explain the increasing female readership. First, the rise of the graphic novel over the last two decades and the growth of webcomics over the past few years have given female (and all) readers far more choices in comics style and content. Second, more publishers—and more women artists—are targeting female readers. For example, English translations of shojo manga (Japanese girls' comics) like X/1999 Sonata and Rg Veda, from the four-woman design team known as CLAMP, are extremely popular with middle school and high school girls. And three, advocacy groups like Friends of Lulu and Sequential Tart work tirelessly to boost female readership and female involvement in all aspects of the comics industry.

Field Sketch: Crossing Gender Lines

I'm a librarian at a K–5 school with a huge population of second language learners, mainly Latino students. Overall library circulation went way up after introducing comics about five years ago. All grades are reading them, both boys and girls, with a lot of students crossing traditional gender lines. For example, boys are reading Archie and Betty & Veronica and girls are reading superheroes like Batman. Second language students at all English levels gravitate toward the comics. The visuals really help! Students get excited by the comics. I remember one fifth-grade boy, a hard-to-reach kid, a real reluctant reader, begging me for all the issues of Bone. It makes quite a difference when you give students what they want to read! Some teachers who were originally against having comics in the library have changed attitude. They have seen the positive effects of comics on students' reading skills and overall interest in reading.

—Carolyn Accatino, Librarian
Meadow Homes Elementary School
Concord, California

Again, this is the readership picture in the United States. Change countries, say to Japan or Mexico, and the picture changes to include many more female readers.

Where can I find a good selection of comics?

Your best bet is your local comics shop. There are about thirty-five hundred shops in the United States. To find one, call The Comic Shop Locator Service toll free at 1-888-266-4226. The same service is online at *<http://csls.diamondcomics.com/>*. Punch in a zip code and you'll quickly have the names, addresses, and phone numbers of your three closest shops. To locate additional stores in the United States as well as comics shops in other countries, try

The Master List of Comic Book and Trading Card Stores at <http://www.the-master-list.com/>.

Shop owners know their comics and are teacher-friendly. Joe Field, of Flying Colors Comics in Concord, California, is a great example. If you let Joe know you're a teacher, he'll take you on a guided tour of the shop and help you find comics in specific genres and with appropriate readability levels. Joe also makes presentations to school faculties and shows examples of various titles for possible use across the curriculum.

Until you've spent some time in comics shops, you may well need a little help in finding what you're looking for. Unlike bookstores that organize by subject and author within subject, comics shops group most of their titles by publisher: DC, Marvel, Fantagraphics, Dark Horse, and the like. Because the by-publisher shelves contain multiple genres, it's easy to miss some great comics unless you've got the time to pick through hundreds of titles.

Most shops have a children's section for the under twelve set. Though upper-grade and adult-school teachers may have the tendency to pass this section up, please don't. You may find something here that interests—and profits—your beginning- to early-intermediate-level students. If you can't get to a comics shop, the next best bet is online ordering. Once you've located a friendly cyberstore, take a virtual tour though the comics aisles and use that plastic money!

Nearly all public and many school libraries have comics. The variety and number of titles, however, vary widely, usually in direct relationship to how comics-friendly and how comics-aware library staff are. Some of the chain bookstores like Borders and Barnes and Noble have small graphic novel sections. The key word here is "small." Once you've seen what's available in a full-fledged comics shop—real or virtual—you'll likely skip the chains. Many independent and used bookstores also have graphic novel sections. But again, the selection is very limited. By the way, be prepared for the occasional mix-up when asking bookstore staff where you can find the graphic novel section. Most employees will know the genre, but not all. One young fellow in a used bookstore in San Diego suggested I try the adult book shop a few blocks north.

Unfortunately, the worst place to look for comics is where anyone old enough to remember hula hoops and 45 RPM records used to buy them: newsstands and drugstores. Check a newsstand or drugstore today and if you're lucky, maybe you'll find a Looney Tunes and an Archie's Pals & Gals for sale. Maybe.

Cost and Durability

What do comics cost?

The average single-issue comic costs around $3.00. Trade paperbacks, larger softbound titles often collecting an entire story run of single issues, run anywhere from $13.00 to $15.00. Teachers on a tight budget, think used. And by used, I don't mean the vintage, collectible comics, some of which can set you back an entire salary check. A few will take an entire year's salary. By used, I mean comics in the $.25 to $1.50 range. You'll often find used comics at this price in comics shops, especially during sales.

The best way to stock a classroom with comics on the cheap, however, is to pick them up at garage sales, fleamarkets, and thrift shops. A fourth-grade teacher told me she bought over a hundred comics for under ten dollars at a church bazaar. I keep hoping I'll hit a garage sale and find a 1938 Action Comics No. 1 featuring the first appearance of Superman for a quarter. A No. 1 recently sold for nearly $90,000 ("Cage Sells Comics Collection" 2002). So far no luck, but I regularly find lots of great low-cost comics for the teachers and students I work with. By the way, save your ninety grand; you can read every page of Action Comics No. 1 online at *<xroads.virginia.edu/~1930s/PRINT/comics.html>*.

Comics seem pretty flimsy. Do they hold up?

The standard, single-issue comic will be dog-eared, ripped, and shot in a month, if it's a popular title that freely circulates in the hands of lower-grade kids. You'll get a little more mileage out of it in the upper grades. With single issues, regardless of grade, keep a big roll of clear packing tape at the ready. Softbound trades, bound instead of stapled like single issues and printed on better paper, will last as long as any other paperback in your classroom library. That said, don't be surprised if the comic trades wear out considerably faster than their non-comic counterparts, not because the comics are made with substandard materials, but because students are reading them more.

Readability

Can I find comics for my low-, mid-, and high-end L2 readers?

Yes, if you're willing to genre hop. It's much tougher to find all the readability levels you need when sticking with one type of material, say western comics or furries (animal strips). With activities that cut across genres, with "Adopt-A-Strip" (see Chapter 3), for example, where students choose a favorite strip and track and share plot developments over several weeks, locating titles at various text levels is little problem.

There are comics for emerging, developing, struggling, and near-native-proficient readers. Comics range from laid-back easy to big-sweat difficult and everything in between. Text-to-picture ratio, the average amount of written text per page or panel in a comic, varies widely. As a general rule, as it varies, so does vocabulary load and the number and complexity of grammar structures.

Comics come wordless, like Gon (see Figure 3–7) and The System; text-light, as in Climbing Out (Figure 2–3) and X/1999 Sonata; text-medium, like WJHC: On the Air! (see Figure 4–7a & b) and The Yellow Jar; or text-heavy, as in Raymond Chandler's Philip Marlowe: The Little Sister and the Age of Bronze series (see Figure 2–4).

Consider the reading span in newspaper comics. Based on the number and range of words per strip, Wright and Sherman (1994) determined the readability grade levels of over six dozen daily comics. Average levels ran from a low of 1.8 (Gasoline Alley and Mickey Mouse) to a high of 7.3 (Tank McNamara). Garfield weighed in at 2.3, Amazing Spider-Man at 4.1, and Doonesbury at 6.4. An earlier analysis (Wright 1979) looked at comic books and found a similar spread, from a low of 1.8 for Archie to a high of 6.4 for Batman and Superman. A strip like Sylvia or Pearls Before Swine, and many graphic novels, like Moore and Campbell's *From Hell* or Art Spiegelman's Pulitzer prize–winning *Maus*, are written at a much higher reading level, have more text, and provide a challenging read for more proficient high school, college, and adult readers.

FIG. 2–3 *From* Climbing Out *by Brian Ralph. Copyright © 2002 by Brian Ralph. Reprinted by permission of Highwater Books, <www.highwaterbooks.com/index.html>.*

How accurate are those official comics readability levels?

About as accurate as official weather forecasts. They give us a starting point and that's about it. The Weather Channel says there's a chance of rain tomorrow and we throw an umbrella in the car just in case.

FIG. 2–4 *From* Age of Bronze: A Thousand Ships *(vol. 1) by Eric Shanower. Copyright ©*
2001 by Eric Shanower. Published by Image Comics, <www.age-of-bronze.com>.
Reprinted by permission of the author. All rights reserved.

Wright and Sherman peg Garfield at 2.3, and if we've got some kids reading at about a second-grade level, we might start with Garfield. But before anyone runs out and loads up on 2.3 Garfield or 6.4 issues of The Dark Knight (a.k.a., Batman), let's post three caveats:

One, the readability measures cited above were based on what's readable for native English speakers, not second language learners. Obviously, "grade-level" comics that are an easy to challenging read for native speakers at a given grade can be a tough to near impossible read for students new to English at the same or even higher grade level.

Two, readability measures are inherently limited because they fail to factor in readers' schemata—background knowledge that helps us process, order, and make sense of the world, including the world in comics. Prior life experiences related to the content of our reading make that content more understandable, more readable; fewer experiences, lower readability.

And three, it's important to remember that the readability measures were determined on words alone, not on words and pictures. In comics, pictures support the words, making the written text more comprehensible.

So, take readability levels with a grain of salt?

Better yet, a whole shaker. Comic text that appears well above the "just-right" independent reading level of a second language learner may be far more readable than expected, if the student is interested in the comic, has prior knowledge about the content, and if there are plenty of visual clues to aid comprehension. Conversely, comic text that appears at or a bit below the "just-right" level may be a more difficult read in the absence of interest, background information, and good pictures. Of course, we can't assume that all students know how to read the pictures, even when they're good.

Some students can't read the pictures?

Right. In fact, many teachers can't read the pictures, or better said, don't take the time to read the pictures. As a longtime comics reader, this surprised me when I first began doing comics activities in staff development workshops. During our twenty-minute block for individual reading, teachers often zoomed through comics at the speed of light. Others thumbed through titles from back to front, as you would a *People* or *Sports Illustrated* magazine while sitting in a dental office waiting for a cavity check. Pictures and picture sequence were frequently slighted and disregarded.

I soon learned to preface comics activities with an anecdote about a first-grade boy I observed some years ago. The little boy was lying on the classroom rug, absorbed in a picture book. I sat beside him and began reading along, letting him turn the pages when he was ready. He moved through the book at a snail's pace, his eyes and fingers lingering over every picture.

At one point, he looked up at me and asked—perhaps echoing the words of his teacher—if I was "reading the pictures." I assured him I was and that I was taking time to read all parts of the pictures so I didn't miss anything. He smiled and signaled his approval with an "OK," and we continued reading, milking the pictures for all they were worth.

Do the pictures in comics guarantee basic comprehension?

I wish they did. Wordless comics aside, pictures help with comprehension and typically provide a significant boost, but unfortunately never guarantee it. How much help pictures offer depends in large part on the ratio of pictures to text—how much of the story is told with art versus how much with words. Beginning second language learners rely on—and require—lots of pictures to get the story; students with more L2 literacy generally require fewer pictures. That much is obvious. What may be less obvious is the fact that comprehension, especially for beginning and many intermediate students, depends not just on the quantity of pictures in a comic, but on the type of pictures. Details matter.

So I could have a picture-heavy comic that bombs?

You sure could. Picture detail, like comic content and text length and density, runs the gamut from stick-figure sparse to full-bodied lush to comics with more detail than an IRS audit. Some pictures consistently and directly support and clarify the narrative; they quite literally illustrate the text. Other pictures offer the reader only occasional and indirect support. Depending on the comic activity and how much comprehension is needed for success with the activity, the amount and type of picture detail can be critical.

For example, let's imagine we've got beginning to intermediate English readers and comics with light to medium amounts of text. Students read individually, then do a mini–book talk, summarizing the comic for their classmates in small groups. To summarize successfully, they'll need at least a moderate level of comprehension, and reaching that level will take plenty of picture detail to illuminate the story line. What if those details are missing? Let's take a look at a talking head strip (Figure 2–5), a type of comic typically short on visual clues. Though the visuals show who's talking (Pig and Zebra), they offer no help with the critical aspect of the strip—the content, what Pig and Zebra are talking about. Better visuals, not in the artistic sense (I love Stephan Pastis' drawings!), but in terms of detail and a closer visual-to-text match, help students grasp more content.

For example, in Jason Lutes' *Jar of Fools*, details of clothing (a frayed jacket), personal hygiene (unkempt hair, beard stubble), and living conditions (cluttered apartment, chipped wall paint) help readers understand the basic who, what, where, when, and why of the graphic novel's down-on-his-luck protagonist. Pick up another comic where the artist-author has chosen to tell a story with a sparser visual style or with more written text, and second language learners may not have the visual detail they need for adequate comprehension. Not all visuals are created equal.

FIG. 2–5 *From* Pearls Before Swine *by Stephan Pastis. Copyright © 2002 by Stephan Pastis. Reprinted by permission of United Feature Syndicate, Inc.*

Does that mean we've got to check every comic's visual-to-text match before using it?!

Only if you're a teacher with no life beyond school. The rest of us may do the occasional checking, say when we're after that just-right comic strip for an overhead modeling on affixes or multiple word meanings. But most of the time, it's the students who do the checking. When given the choice and a wide range of comics to choose from, students will gravitate to comics they find comprehensible, that make sense.

Isn't there a danger that students will read the pictures and skip the words?

Not if they want the whole story. And they'll want the whole story if it's a compelling story. With most comics—other than wordless comics, of course—if you don't read the words you don't get the story, or at best you get only a small part of the story. Naturally, students with lower second language reading skills rely more on the pictures for making meaning. Using the visuals is a smart reading strategy. I used it repeatedly in the fall of 2002 while teaching in mainland China and shopping for essentials at a market and a pharmacy. My skill in Chinese reading is only a little better than my skill in piloting a commercial jetliner, which is to say, near nonexistent. Beyond the characters for hotel, restaurant, and men's room, I'm at a loss. Reading the pictures enabled me to buy bottled water instead of carpet cleaner and toothpaste instead of itch cream.

Yet even students with beginning-level L2 reading skills will tackle some written text along with the visuals, assuming, again, a high-interest comic and especially if students are experienced comics readers in L1.

Have a lot of ESL students read comics in their first language?

Tons. If you have students from Japan, it's almost guaranteed. Between 90 and 95 percent of all literate Japanese read comics, the highest comics readership of any country in the world. Large numbers of students from Mexico will also be comic book literate. In Mexico, around 70 percent of readers read comics (Mayfield, Mayfield, and

Genestre 2001). In a fascinating political history of comics in Mexico, Anne Rubenstein (1998) confirms the huge readership: "Historietas [comic books] are tremendously popular (even in 1990, after two decades of declining circulation, eight of the ten best-selling periodicals were comic books), and their popularity cuts across lines of region, age, gender, and even class" (p. 8).

The number of comics readers in other countries, like France, Italy, Korea, and Taiwan, though not as substantial, is still high compared to the relatively low U.S. readership (not counting newspaper strip readers). U.S. estimates vary widely. Brent Frankenhoff, managing editor of *Comics Buyer's Guide,* pegs the number of comic book readers at 1 to 1.5 million ("Hey Kids, a New Holiday!" 2003). Other industry experts like Joe Field of Flying Colors Comics in Concord, California, estimate U.S. readership at 3 to 4 million (personal communication 2004).

How does experience with comics in L1 help students read comics in L2?

Experienced comics readers know the form, the basic conventions used in drawing and writing comics. For example, they know the difference between thought and dialogue balloons. They know that large, non-bubbled text is typically a sound effect and that a string of nonsense symbols like #?"@?#*?! isn't nonsense at all but an unprintable obscenity that could make a sailor blush. Wavy lines signal movement or smoke. Add flies to the wavy lines and you've got a rotten smell. Comics readers know that a dotted body outline indicates invisibility and "X's" on eyes equal unconsciousness or death. They know you've got to read between the panels for missing information. And most important, they understand that visual text and written text are interdependent, working together to inform, spin a tale, make a joke, or in the case of the best horror comics, scare the stuffing out of you. Even our young, less experienced readers often reveal an awareness of comics conventions. Benjamin Li, one of Kia Foster's second graders at Kitayama Elementary School in Union City, California, clearly understands the difference between dialogue and thought balloons (see Figure 2–6).

Proficient comics readers take the time to read the pictures and the words. Because most comics conventions are universal across languages, conventions learned with first language comics makes

FIG. 2–6 *Thinking of Love. Benjamin Li, grade 2, Kitayama Elementary, Union City, California.*

reading comics in the second language easier. Easier, but certainly not a breeze, especially when we consider our beginning-level L2 readers.

What can comics do for my highly reluctant L2 readers?

Get them reading for a start. And keep them reading if we use the right comics. Readability is determined in part by the amount of text per page and the total number of those pages in a selection. This word-count factor is especially critical for early intermediate to intermediate second language learners asked to read page after page of grade-level text containing hundreds and hundreds of unknown words.

I'm an intermediate-level reader in Spanish, my second language. I can comprehend—and enjoy—short magazine and newspaper articles. But give me a 300-page mystery novel and I'll be lucky to make it past page 5 knowing I've got another 295 pages staring me in the face. The task of dealing with that many pages filled with so many stumbling-block words is simply too daunting. I'm worn out before the detective even reaches the murder scene. Add some pictures, however, and I'll dig in, reading captions and some of the nearby text. Add lots and lots of pictures, as with comics, and I may go the distance—if I'm interested in what I'm reading.

So comics help fight L2 learner fatigue?

Help, yes, but they don't knock it out completely, of course. I'm still a bit fatigued after reading a Bolillo and a Vaquero, two of my favorite comics from Mexico, and both have manageable amounts of text and plenty of helpful pictures. Making meaning in a second language is no easy feat. But without the text reduction and visuals, I'm shot. So are a lot of our second language students. Large amounts of written text overwhelm beginning L2 readers and can soon tire and demoralize intermediate and even early advanced readers.

Overwhelm and demoralize? L2 reading gets that bad?

It can. Unfortunately, lots of teachers have forgotten what it's like to be overwhelmed and demoralized by L2 reading. Most of the teachers I work with haven't done any sustained second language reading since their last high school or college foreign language class.

In workshops and university courses, to give teachers a feel for what many of our second language learners experience with L2 reading, I'll bring in some native-level short stories written in languages other than English: Spanish, French, Italian, German, Mandarin, Japanese. Teachers choose a story in a language studied in school or one they knew as a child, perhaps, but later lost, then take the story home to read on their own.

I ask them to spend an hour—if possible— making as much sense of the story as they can. Some use bilingual dictionaries, some use context clues, and others a combination of the two to get the reading done. In follow-up discussions, most teachers report that they stay with the reading from ten to thirty minutes, then call it a day. Few, except those with higher levels of literacy in the target language, last the full hour; It's just too frustrating to do all the dictionary and context guessing work and still miss large portions of the story.

So the teachers feel the same pain as their second language students?

Not quite. As we discuss the L2 reading, teachers admit how tough and tedious the assignment was and declare an enhanced or newfound empathy for students tackling text in a second language. But they also acknowledge that what they experienced is only mildly comparable to what their

> ### Field Sketch: Tintin to the Rescue
>
> I tutored a Spanish Immersion student, an English speaker, going into third grade a couple summers ago. His favorite books in the world were Tintin. He was a very reluctant Spanish speaker—could do it, but claimed to "hate" Spanish. So I found him Tintin in Spanish, and he just had the best time figuring out who all the characters were and what the catchphrases and jokes were in Spanish. It was the most motivated I'd ever seen him. His mom said he even voluntarily picked it up, which never happened with any other Spanish text. I Xeroxed a few of the strips, whiting out the print, and had him write them. He enjoyed that too, and especially wanted to go back and compare what he'd written to the "real" words.
>
> —Deborah Palmer, Doctoral Student
> Language, Literacy, and Cultures in Education
> University of California at Berkeley
> Berkeley, California

> ### Field Sketch: Why I Read Comics
>
> The comic books [comic strip reprints] . . . are esy to red because they have pictures and they are funy, interesting. and the best thing is that they are short. [unedited comments]
>
> —Jesús Gaona, Freshman
> Elsie Allen High School
> Santa Rosa, California

students experience. The workshop or university reading assignment is voluntary, short, and ungraded. Make it more like school—mandatory, long, and worth a letter grade and a notch up or down in self-esteem—and you come closer to reality for second language learners.

Whenever possible, I follow the first reading assignment with a second, this time using comics in several languages. Teachers move from tedium to challenge, from sinking to swimming (or at least floating) in second language text. They read for longer periods of time. And many use the same word students use to describe their comics experience: fun.

Some of my native English speakers read lots of translated Japanese comics. Are these titles workable for second language learners as well?

Manga, the Japanese term for comics, are especially workable. All things being equal, specifically genre and age of target audience, manga titles are generally text-lighter than their American counterparts, often significantly lighter (see Figure 2–7). Far fewer words per page make the comics a natural with students new to English reading.

Manga titles, first published in Japan, are adapted by U.S. publishers like Dark Horse Comics or VIZ for the English-speaking market. The publishers—and let's thank them and the ESL gods for this!—use native English speakers as translators. This means we're spared travel menu English, as in "break apart cattle" for "shredded beef" and "dropping liquid" for "dipping sauce."

Manga are popular with large numbers of comics readers in this country and you'll find dozens of titles lining the shelves in most comics shops. Japanese comics have inspired and influenced a number of American artists who now draw manga-style—characters with big eyes, small mouths and noses, wild hairdos, and exaggerated body dimensions; and action that often explodes beyond the panel.

Some manga are read front-to-back, others back-to-front. What's going on and what do I use with my L2 students?

Like Hebrew, Arabic, and Farsi (Persian), Japanese is read right to left. For a comic in Japanese, this means starting at what English readers

FIG. 2–7 *From* INUYASHA: A Feudal Fairy Tale *(vol. 1) by Rumiko Takahashi. Copyright ©*
1997 by Rumiko Takahashi/Shogakukan, Inc. First published by Shogakukan, Inc. in Japan as
"Inuyasha." Reprinted by permission of VIZ, <www.viz.com/>.

would call the "back" of the book and reading toward the "front." This right-to-left movement holds panel-to-panel as well as for dialogue and descriptive sections within a single panel. U.S. publishers print what are known as "flopped" or left-to-right versions of manga for English readers. Many English manga editions are flopped, but not all. A growing number of titles, like Dragon Ball Z, Cowboy Bebop, and Paradise Kiss, are translated to English but retain the right-to-left format, staying true to the original layout and giving the comics a more authentic Japanese feel.

Like most teachers I know who are using manga, I've steered clear of the non-flopped, right-to-left variety, believing such a format only muddies the reading waters. Why have students reading right to left when English is read left to right? Why take a chance on even slightly disorienting students while we're working so hard to get them comfortable with the conventions of English reading? Staying with left-to-right manga makes sense for most students, but perhaps not all. A teacher in one workshop told me he used right-to-left titles with a couple ESL fourth graders who were good readers in their native Japanese. The teacher felt the right-to-left format provided a familiar reference point for these students and helped them bridge to English reading.

Do the jokes in lots of comics make them too difficult for my beginning second language learners?

If read alone, yes, even with a good bilingual dictionary at the ready. The puns and sarcasm in The Fusco Brothers, the American teen in-jokes in Zits and Archie, the American business spoofs in Dilbert, or the comic political ironies in Doonesbury, Boondocks, and La Cucaracha make for tough reading. Without a teacher or more English-proficient classmate to mediate, not only will your beginners find joke-heavy comics incomprehensible, some of your intermediate and a few of your advanced learners will too.

Even comics that appear joke-light can be a challenge. Let's take a "simple" single-panel Ziggy cartoon as an example (see Figure 2–8). Getting the joke entails more than comprending the basic text, including the "pulling your leg" idiom, and correctly inferencing that the harried mouse threatened the cat with a lawsuit. The humor, in large part, hinges on understanding the litigious nature of American

FIG. 2–8 *Ziggy by Tom Wilson. Copyright © 1998 Ziggy and Friends, Inc. Reprinted by permission of Universal Press Syndicate. All rights reserved.*

society. Students from home countries where people are not as quick to drag their neighbor to court may miss the joke.

A teacher-facilitated discussion or a "buddy read," where beginners work with native speakers or more advanced L2 learners to get the jokes, can turn a comic that would have been an impenetrable and frustrating read if processed alone into something understandable, funny, and meaningful.

Activities

sometimes tell teachers and my university students that I learned everything I know about teaching from Leticia, an irrepressible little third grader I worked with in my early days in the public schools. It's an overstatement, of course, but not by much. Leticia had little patience with teacher talk. Anytime my oral directions or direct instruction went on too long, Leticia would wave a hand and before I could call on her, shout out, "Let's DO something!" It took me awhile to realize the wisdom in her words. If I could jump into a time machine and go back and redo those first few years of teaching, I'd make sure I taught a lot more by doing and a lot less by talking.

With Leticia and several other million talked-to-death students around the world in mind, this chapter answers the DOING question: What can students DO with comics? It offers twenty-five comics-based activities for actively engaging second language learners across the grades and across the curriculum. Each major activity is divided into five parts:

1. Materials (type of comics needed)
2. Description (a brief description of what students do)
3. Topics and Strategies (highlighted per activity)

4. Background (information on key instructional topics)
5. Process (steps and hints on implementation)

Following the major activities, you'll find a section called "Quick Takes" containing a number of additional spin-off activities described in brief.

Though the activities help develop a significant number of second language skills, all are communication based rather than skills based. Each uses cartoons, comic strips, comic books, or graphic novels for real communication purposes. So students, from kindergarten rugrats to middle-aged immigrants at adult ed centers, *do* something with the comics—they laugh, cry, and argue about them, think, talk, draw, and write about them with one another. As they do all that, they build skills. But *why* they do all that is not to get skills; they engage with comics because they want to communicate something funny, poignant, interesting, or important about the content of the comics.

All the activities integrate the four macro skills of listening, speaking, reading, and writing, though some activities clearly foster more receptive (listening and reading) or expressive (speaking and writing) skills. Nearly all are collaborative in nature, designed for pairs or small groups in order to increase student-to-student talk and peer assistance. And all the activities have legs, traveling easily up and down the grades with only minor teacher tweaking.

Finally, each activity can be referenced to—and help students meet—a wide range of content and ELD (English language development) standards. Assessing how well students meet those standards is a natural part of each activity, rather than a separate, add-on task. Both product (what students create) and process (how students create it) can be assessed. How much you assess will depend on the number and type of standards targeted.

Make-A-Title

Materials: cartoons and comic strips

Description: Students work in pairs and create a title for a comic.

Topics and Strategies:
- title as an abstract
- building critical thinking skills
- teacher modeling
- passive versus active talking
- "shrinking title" route
- pairing for language help

Background

Comic books and graphic novels come with titles. The fact that most cartoons and comic strips don't is a blessing in disguise for language teachers and anyone interested in helping students build critical thinking skills. A title, or "abstract" in narrative text analysis (Hatch 1992), boils a story down to its essence. Getting to that essence requires basic story comprehension, identification of main ideas, and a synthesis of those ideas into a phrase or single word that unifies and represents the whole.

Process

With Make-A-Title, like so many activities, teacher modeling is the key. Consider the FoxTrot comic (Figure 3–1). If students are asked to work in pairs and create a title that tells what the comic is about, we might get:

> Guys Playing
> Guys on the Wall
> Pool of Lava
> Snakes and Alligators
> Cooties

With some whole-class modeling, where students listen in on how the teacher and a volunteer student pool background and language knowledge, use visual clues, determine key ideas, and come up with an accurate title, we're more likely to get titles related to the strip's main idea: young boys' dislike (or pretend dislike) for girls. One pair of fifth-grade second language learners—after modeling—recently dubbed this comic "Boys Scared of Girls."

In the modeling and in reminders offered by the teacher during pair work, students learn the difference between passive and active talking, the difference between talking *to* one another:

FIG. 3–1 FoxTrot by Bill Amend. Copyright © 2000 by Bill Amend. Reprinted by permission of Universal Press Syndicate. All rights reserved.

A: It's about two boys.
B: They are on a wall. And a girl.
A: They say, "pool of lava" and "snakes."
B: He says, "cooties."
A: Let's call the title "Boys Wall Cooties."

and talking *with* one another:

A: It's about two boys. Who is this? (*pointing to boy shaking*).
B: I think Jason. He sees a girl and shakes. Scared. Maybe scared?
A: Yeah, scared, like snakes and alligators!
B: Is the other boy scared? What is cooties?
A: I don't know. (*to a classmate*) What is cooties?

Conversations without modeling and reminders are often conversations in name only. Students tell what they know and describe what they see. With modeling and reminders, conversations are typically more active. Students move beyond simple description and ask each other many more questions about the comic. They co-construct a title after a lot of meaning-making efforts rather than simply "lifting" a title from the comic's surface language and visuals.

Getting on to the concept of an "abstract" takes some time for lower-grade students. These kids may end up with titles containing more words than the cartoon or strip itself. You get a story—the whole story—not an abstract. A "shrinking title" route, as a model and during guided practice, often helps students struggling with the boil-down process. Students begin with a full sentence, then whittle that down to a phrase and sometimes to a single word.

Titling can also be difficult for beginning L2 learners in the upper grades who understand the concept, but may have little language to use beyond what appears in the strip. The result is shorter but often inaccurate titles. These students may need to pair with native speakers or more advanced L2 classmates to get the additional vocabulary they need to move beyond the given text.

Though I've done the activity with each pair of students working with a different cartoon or strip, I prefer having several pairs titling the same comic. Once the titles are finished, we've got a lot more to discuss—and debate!—regarding which pair really "nailed" the title.

I sometimes do this activity as a tie-in to a student-made comics activity like Take-A-Stand (see p. 110). Titling commercial comics gives students a chance to gain some of the conceptual and language skills they'll need for accurately titling their own editorial cartoons.

Add-A-Panel

Materials: comic strips

Description: Students expand a strip's story line with their own panels.

Topics and Strategies:
- predicting while reading
- learning comprehension stategies while learning language
- importance of text reduction
- student-made comics as popular reading

Background

This activity hinges on students' ability to make logical predictions. Proficient readers continually predict as they move through text. Prediction, a type of inferencing, keeps us engaged in what we're reading and helps us make better sense of the text (Anderson and Pearson 1984; Keene and Zimmermann 1997). What we may fail to appreciate as adult native speakers, however, is that our predictions are possible because we understand all or nearly all the words we're reading. Few second language learners have that advantage as they read in L2.

Young early readers as well as older students who are non- or semi-literate in their first language are often asked to do double duty: learn a fundamental reading skill like predicting while also learning the meanings of the words needed to exercise that skill, in this case making those predictions. The reduced, pictured-supported text in comics makes the comprehension job and, hence, the prediction job a lot easier.

FIG. 3–2 Mutts by Patrick McDonnell. Copyright © 1996 by Patrick McDonnell. Reprinted by special permission of King Features Syndicate.

Process

With Add-A-Panel, I typically have elementary-grade students add a single "what happens next?" panel to a strip. Steven Jaurigui, one of teacher Pamela Heyda's second graders in San Mateo, California, took a Mutts strip (Figure 3–2) and added a panel featuring a very hungry dinosaur (Figure 3–3a). Working with the same comic, classmate Hannie Hararah showed the next logical action: heading to the store for food (see Figure 3–3b). Some students, however, like second grader Quang Pham in teacher Kia Foster's class in Union City, California, may add several panels (Figure 3–4, and Figure 3–5), extending the story with another full installment. Middle school through adult ESL students sometimes like to serialize a favorite base strip. Some of the story arcs from older students can run to a dozen or more three-panel "chapters."

For the inevitable "I-can't-draw!" students, I'll model a panel or two with basic stick figures or suggest that the strip's illustrations be used as drawing guides. If the activity is done in pairs, art-anxious students can turn to their partner for drawing help.

Expanded strips are popular reading items. At the end of the activity, expect a flurry of strip trading around the classroom. Though I usually offer a choice of strips, I sometimes have all students add on to the same strip. Students enjoy reading their classmates' different takes on the comic, and the variations in story line and language provide lots of grist for the discussion mill.

Another option worth exploring is a class strip. One student adds a panel to the "starter" strip and then passes it to another student, who adds a second frame. The strip continues to circulate around the classroom (or expand at a center) until every student has had a chance to contribute. Panels can be completed after students have finished other work or taken home to be worked on and shared and discussed with parents. Some strips are finished in a day; others develop more slowly and might take a couple weeks to complete. Added

I think a dinosaur
eats all the food
and they go to
the store.

FIG. 3–3a *Hungry Dinosaur. Steven Jaurigui, grade 2, Horrall Elementary, San Mateo, California.*

They are going to
the grocery store to
bye some dog food.

FIG. 3–3b *Trip to the Store. Hannie Hararah, grade 2, Horrall Elementary, San Mateo, California.*

FIG.3–4 *Mutts by Patrick McDonnell. Copyright © 1996 by Patrick McDonnell. Reprinted by special permission of King Features Syndicate.*

FIG. 3–5 *Busting the Lamp. Quang Pham, grade 2, Kitayama Elementary, Union City, California.*

panels can be assessed in terms of the degree to which they logically extend the strip's story line.

Fill-It-Up

Materials: comic strips

Description: Students create dialogue and captions for comics with deleted text.

Topics and Strategies:
- literacy as number one skill
- skill integration over skill separation
- day-one literacy over literacy shielding

- reasonable literacy demands
- making sense rule
- reading the pictures
- cloze assessment

Background

Put a hundred teachers in a room and ask what makes a school successful and you'll get a hundred different answers, everything from a safe working environment, classroom Web access, student respect, and relevant curriculum, to peer coaching, fair compensation, supporting the primary language, a full-time librarian, a visionary principal, and involved parents. Ask what makes a student successful and teachers think, "skills."

When I pose the second question in staff development workshops, the answers usually boil down to four or five key skill areas: literacy, math, problem solving, interpersonal relations, and learning/study skills. If I then ask teachers to pick the one skill students must have to do well in school, the one they absolutely can't live without, the unanimous choice is always literacy—even in a room filled with mostly math and science teachers.

The literacy choice is no mystery. Teachers know that all content areas involve reading and writing and that the reading-writing load increases as students move up the grades. Literacy skills alone, of course, won't guarantee school success; their absense, however, routinely means school failure. Teachers also know that students with high-level literacy will have many more options in the marketplace than students with low-level skills. In and out of school, literacy is a student's "ticket to ride."

How do we make sure our second language learners get tickets? One way is to favor skill integration over skill separation. An integrated approach avoids the traditional ESL practice of separating language into four distinct worlds of listening, speaking, reading, and writing. Teachers favoring integration design activities where students use—and thus develop—all four modes as they complete their task or project.

With an integrated approach, our second language beginners deal with written text from day one, a far cry from traditional "literacy shielding," which delays the introduction of reading and writing until students have attained a certain level of oral skills. David and Yvonne Freeman (2001) remind us that delaying L2 literacy carries a huge downside: students fall behind their native-speaking peers in academic content learning. The literacy demands on L2 beginners must be reasonable, of course. We want to engage them in reading and writing, not overwhelm them. Fill-It-Up provides beginners with a reasonable quantity of text to read and write.

The puzzle aspect of the activity—creating dialogue that completes the strip—challenges students at all proficiency levels. Moreover, all levels can succeed with the activity since appropriate, "puzzle-solving" dialogue and caption description are readily available. Students can use their existing stockpile of language, borrow vocabulary and structures from surrounding text in the strip to be filled (or from other strips by the same artist), and turn to peers and teacher for language help.

Process

Students work individually or in pairs with comic strips missing various amounts of dialogue. A Jane's World strip, for example, might have two of its five dialogue balloons blank. A Liberty Meadows might have all the dialogue deleted. The task is to replace the missing text and complete the strip. The primary guideline for students on dialogue creation: What goes into a balloon must make sense. The making-sense rule helps minimize the following type of exchange: Character One asks, "Where's the horse?" and Character Two answers in replacement text, "I love Gamecube games!" The phrase I use with students over and over again as I model text that works—or doesn't—is that our words must "make, not break, the story."

Beginners have the easiest time with strips where all the dialogue is deleted. They've got lots of balloons to fill, but they can fill them and still make a complete story using their limited linguistic resources. In contrast, text-heavy strips with only one balloon blank present a much more challenging read and write. Students must be able to comprehend the existing text, perhaps several reading levels above them, then create replacement text—if it's to make sense—using vocabulary and structures few if any beginners would have.

Even the strips with all the text deleted, however, must be read. Students are reading their own words, of course, but they're also reading the pictures, examining each for clues that dictate and guide the creation of their replacement text. Beginners commonly fill their balloons with only a word or two. Yet for all students, regardless of L2 proficiency, the expectation still holds: the strip must make sense. Without a detailed reading of the visuals, beginners can easily end up with "broken" nonsense stories.

Some hints on logistics. Deleting dialogue takes time. You'll want to delete text from a couple strips for modeling purposes, but beyond the models, have the students do all the deleting. Each student locates a comic and deletes a certain amount of text per teacher direction. Depending on students' language proficiency and our language targets, various amounts of text can be deleted, from one or two words, to a sentence or two, to all words in an entire panel or strip. For example, with an aim to improve students' use of prepositions, a Peanuts strip featuring Snoopy as the World War I flying ace (from *Around the World in 45 Years: Charlie Brown's Anniversary Celebration,* by Charles Schulz [1994]) might read:

CHARLIE BROWN: You're late. We've already started eating.
SNOOPY: There was heavy fighting [deleted] St. Mihiel.
CHARLIE BROWN: Linus is having dinner [deleted] us tonight.
LINUS: Why is he [Snoopy] looking [deleted] me so funny?
SNOOPY: I'm not used to eating [deleted] the enlisted men.

A middle school teacher I recently worked with had her intermediate-level L2 learners delete every third word in their Fill-It-Up strips. The strips became a type of informal cloze test used to assess reading comprehension. After deleting, students exchange modified strips. Make sure students save a copy of the base strip with all the original text in place. At the end of the activity, most students will want to compare and contrast their creations with the artist's original work.

The easiest way to delete is on the computer. Students cut a strip from a comics website, paste it into a draw or paint document, then quickly remove dialogue using an erase tool. Strips are printed out and ready for filling. When computer deleting isn't possible, try black-out. Students use black markers or dark crayons to eliminate dialogue in comics snipped from newspapers. The hardest way to delete is with liquid white-out. It's costly, messy, and time inefficient. I don't recommend it at all, especially with elementary kids who end up whiting out their hands and clothing as often as their comics.

Unless students are cutting and pasting new dialogue into strips via computer, fitting text into small balloons is an often impossible task. Students with tiny, neat printing can sometimes manage it. So can beginning L2 students who fill with minimal text. Everybody else, and that may well mean your entire class, must move beyond the bubble (and caption) boundaries. Students might begin a line of dialogue in a balloon, then finish up outside the balloon and even outside the panel. A neater, more readable option is to have students number their balloons. Text corresponding to each number is written above or below the strip. Teachers with access to good copy machines have another possibility: enlarging the strips. Bigger balloons are much easier to write in.

A note on scheduling: Fill-It-Up generally requires less class time than the more ambitious Missing Panels (see p. 88), since students replace only the text, not text and pictures.

Scripting

Material: wordless comics

Description: In pairs, students read wordless comics and create oral and written scripts.

Topics and Strategies:
- pair work
- importance of using engaging comics
- compliance talk versus dialogue
- fishbowl modeling
- narrative template
- inferencing (reading between the panels)
- reciprocal teaching

Background

Pair activities provide lots of interaction and, therefore, lots of opportunities for oral language building. Or so the theory goes. Unfortunately, pairs don't automatically talk and work well together. The "pair work" issue surfaces frequently in my travels as a teacher coach. For those teachers working hard to decrease teacher talk and increase student-to-student talk, the issue is especially important. As one middle school history teacher put it, "If I've got dead, non-working pairs, I just go back to lecturing."

Process

Here are two hints for avoiding the "deadly duo" phenomenon and getting your pairs to chat and produce with Scripting. Hint One: Use engaging comics. If I'm asked to read a boring comic, you could pair me with anybody, including the comic's creator, and I'm not going to chat much. I may talk, especially if I'm a tenth grader and there's a grade involved, but not a lot. If my partner is feeling the same way about the material, interaction will be minimal and our script will be ho-hum at best. An engaging comic can move pairs from compliance talk—talk to satisfy the teacher—to lively and creative dialogue.

> ### Field Sketch: Oral Language Boost
>
> I sometimes give small groups of students a set of cut-out comic strip panels without text and have them arrange the panels the way they want. Then they either fill in the dialogue and captions, or use the pictures as a basis for a longer, written story. Finally, I make a transparency of their finished comic and they present it to the class. This activity can be used with students from beginner to advanced levels. The activity produces a large amount of oral language as the students discuss the arrangement of the panels and the dialogue/story line elements.
>
> —Kathy Javdani, ESL Teacher
> Mt. Diablo High School
> Concord, California

What interests teachers, of course, doesn't always interest students. Those wordless Peter Kuper comics (*Eye of the Beholder*) that you find so intriguing and keep recommending to colleagues, friends, and perfect strangers may bore half your middle schoolers to death. Students passing on Kuper, however, may chat and write up a storm if given the chance to work with comics from Sergio Aragonés' *Louder Than Words* (see Figure 3–6). Whenever possible, I try to lay out a variety of comics and let the pairs choose something that grabs them. With the range of wordless titles on the market, you and your students will have plenty to choose from. See the comics review section of Chapter 4 for possibilities.

Hint Two: Model the scripting process, including both descriptive narration and dialogue. For a small class, you might do a "fishbowl" model where you and a student sit at a desk or table and read through a sample comic together, the other students circled around you looking in and listening. With a large class, you're more likely to model the process at the overhead. Keep the modeling brief; ultimately, we want students to spend more time *doing* than watching. I generally model with six to twelve panels. Beyond a dozen we run the risk of modeling overkill. The modeled story can be as simple or as complex as you'd like, depending on students' language proficiency levels.

Read the comic three times. The first time through is a quick read, in silence, to take in the whole of the story. The second is a slightly longer, more detailed read, where you and your student partner comment briefly on story elements and help one another over comprehension trouble spots, for example, "Is that

FIG. 3–6 *From* Louder Than Words *by Sergio Aragonés. Copyright © 1998 by Sergio Aragonés. Published by Dark Horse Comics, Inc.,* <www.darkhorse.com/>. *Reprinted by permission of the publisher.*

the boy's mom in that picture?" "Is she sick or just tired?" "What happened to the brother?" Without the whole, knowing where the story is headed and how it gets there (first read), and without a grasp of what the pictures are showing (second read), it's difficult for students to create a coherent script.

On the third and last time through, use the visual content of each panel to build your story. You can alternate panels with the student or work together on each picture to construct a story line. You might also want to invite the observing students to join you in the story building. Often, no invitation is needed; if students like the comic, they jump right in.

Here's an example of a narration (or voice-over) created by a whole class during a modeling session I did with Nick Jackson's third graders at Hawthorne School in Oakland, California. The comic was a nine-panel story from *Gon on Safari* by Masashi Tanaka, transferred to four overhead transparencies. (See Figure 3–7). As students discussed each transparency, I recorded their ideas on chart paper. A "T" in the transcription indicates a word I contributed to our narration. In the verb splits—for example, are/were—one student provided one word, another student the other. After our first draft, we went back into the text and decided on which verbs we wanted to keep.

PANEL 1: One day, a little dinosaur stood (T) in a forest at the base (T) of a huge tree. He was hungry.
PANEL 2: The tree was full of fruit and bird (T) nests.
PANEL 3: One nest was shake/shaking side to side. Gon was kick/kicking the tree.
PANEL 4: The birds are/were scared because they are/were going to fall.
PANEL 5: Suddenly (T), Gon kick/kicked the tree again (T).
PANEL 6: The tree shakes/shook (T) furiously.
PANEL 7: Fruit fell in Gon's mouth.
PANEL 8: Now (T) he's looking/looked up. He wanted (T) more fruit.
PANEL 9: Boom! Gon is/was furious that the nest fell on his head!

Nick later told me that "furious" was one of the terms on that week's key vocabulary list. Beyond providing students with new or reinforced vocabulary and structures, the activity modeling helps our early-grade students learn the basic narrative template, the conventions of storytelling and story writing: title, time and setting, characters, goal or problem, plan and action steps, and resolution.

Minus the narrative template modeling, many students, even those with higher levels of L2, simply tell what they see in the comic. You'll get panel description, a worthwhile objective—I wish I could describe a comic panel, any panel, in Mandarin!—but not the panel linkage that comes from inferencing, from reading between the panels. Moreover, description "stories," often done in what I call a "then-then" style, typically leave out one or more narrative template items required for a well-told tale. Here's a composite but representative sample of how several students told the same "nest on the head" story in

FIG. 3–7 *From Gon on Safari by Masashi Tanaka. Copyright © 2000 by Masashi Tanaka. Published by Paradox Press, an imprint of DC Comics, <www.dccomics.com/>. Reprinted by permission of DC Comics. All rights reserved.*

another third-grade classroom of L2 learners, this time without the benefit of teacher modeling and mediation. Students worked individually and were simply asked to look at the pictures and make up a story. I've corrected syntax and tense errors.

PANEL 1: There was a dinosaur and a tree.
PANEL 2: The tree had nests.
PANEL 3: Then a nest moved.
PANEL 4: Then the birds were mad.
PANEL 5: Then the dinosaur kicked the tree.

FIG. 3–8a *From* The Motherless One *by Gene Yang. Copyright © 2001 by Gene Yang. Reprinted by permission of the author,* <www.geocities.com/misteryang/>.

PANEL 6: The tree moved.
PANEL 7: Then fruit fell on the dinosaur.
PANEL 8: Then the dinosaur looked.
PANEL 9: Then the nest was on his head.

After the modeling, students work in pairs with other wordless comics, replicating the process: quick read, detailed read, and scripting. Students can also use comics having a mix of scripted and wordless panels (see Figures 3–8a and 3–8b). The scripted panels provide clues, vocabulary, and structures for writing description and dialogue for the wordless frames. The teacher circulates and helps with the picture reading and writing when needed.

FIG. 3–8b *From* The Motherless One *by Gene Yang. Copyright © 2001 by Gene Yang. Reprinted by permission of the author,* <www.geocities.com/misteryang/>.

The process shares elements with reciprocal teaching (RT) (Palincsar and Brown 1984; Carter 1997). RT uses structured teacher- and student-led dialogue to improve reading comprehension. The dialogue focuses on what proficient readers do to build meaning. Teachers trained in this approach may want to revamp the process outlined here to include RT's principal steps during a pair-read:

- summarizing (finding main ideas)
- questioning (generating "self-test" questions)
- clarifying (identifying comprehension breakdowns, making repairs)
- predicting (activating prior knowledge, making "what's next" guesses)

Scripts are typically written out, though teachers short on time or those wanting to work specifically on oral language development sometimes skip the writing. Oral, unscripted narrations can be saved and reviewed via audio recording.

The activity culminates with a sharing of student work. When all students have copies of the comics and can follow along in the visual text, pairs present their narration to the whole class. When multiple copies of comics are unavailable, the written or recorded narrations can be placed at a reading-listening center.

Missing Panels

Materials: comic strips

Description: Students replace missing comics panels with their own creations.

Topics and Strategies:
- narrative cohesion and coherence
- "alone but together" format
- periodic, short writing minilessons
- transfering learning to other curriculum areas

Background

Good stories make sense. Seasoned writers know that making sense depends on cohesion and coherence. Each sentence in a story must logically link to the next (cohesion) and ultimately, all sentences must add up to a meaningful whole (coherence). Emerging and inexperienced writers may be unaware of the need for both elements. Other would-be writers may understand the need for cohesion and coherence, but not have the skills—or the language—to ensure their presence in a narrative. Constructing a good story is a formidable task in your first language; in your second, it's especially daunting.

Process

In this activity, students work with comic strips that are missing one or more panels. The comic might be a four-panel Cathy with the second frame deleted, or several consecutive days of Spider-Man or Tarzan strips with Wednesday's installment missing. Students must create replacement frames for the deleted items so that once the "holes" are filled, the comic makes sense within panels, from panel to panel, and as a unifed whole.

During panel construction, students consider a number of items related to cohesion-coherence, including:

- topic continuity (subject matter flow)
- character continuity (trait maintenance)
- joke template (setup, elaboration, punch line)
- pragmatics (socioculturally appropriate forms)
- tense forms (throw versus threw versus will throw)
- temporal conjunctions (before, after, when)
- temporal adverbials (now, two weeks ago, someday)
- collocations (baggy pants versus big pants)
- lexical chains (shopping . . . mall . . . store)
- antecedent-referent clarity (Lola ate the apple . . . She ate it.)

Beyond the boost to vocabulary and structure acquisition, the activity helps students learn what goes into a comprehensible and compelling narrative. As they create replacement panels, students must attend to what comes *before* and what comes *after* in order to make sure that what comes *now* in a strip—their panel—makes sense. After construction, students share their panels with the class and compare and contrast their work with the strips' published originals.

A few hints for increasing the learning mileage in Missing Panels:

1. Try an "alone but together" format. Though I generally ask for individual work in this activity, with each student drawing and writing his or her own replacement panels, I always seat students in pairs or small groups. The "alone but together" format increases interaction and therefore the chance to use L2, while also providing built-in helpers. Students do "meaning checks" on each other's work during panel construction. When a panel doesn't make sense, the checker identifies the problem spot (Where the girl says "those"), tells why it's a

problem (I don't know if "those" means "cats" or "shoes"), and if needed, suggests a repair (The girl can use the word "cats" again).

2. Offer periodic, short minilessons on difficult items. Asking students to focus on an element of pragmatics, for example, whether a character's use of colloquialisms is appropriate for a given context, may be futile if students are unfamiliar with the range of colloquialisms and their use in various American settings. Mastering the use of colloquialisms, pronoun referents, subject-verb agreement, joke elaboration, or any number of other cohesion-coherence elements takes time—and some help from the teacher.

I do most of my minilessons with this activity on an informal basis, as I make the rounds from group to group. I might hit a dozen or so different grammatical or lexical issues within a forty- to sixty-minute session, but work on only a couple items with any one student or group. I give examples of dialogue and description that make (and break) panel cohesion or strip unity, occasionally draw and write model panels, and usually pose the "Does this make sense?" question a thousand times a session. At least it feels like a thousand!

When I find an item giving most students a problem, I'll do a minilesson at the overhead for the entire class using student- and teacher-drawn comic samples. Character continuity is a good example of an item that's frequently troublesome throughout the grades. Students will "break character" in their panels, suddenly having someone speak in a manner that contradicts established traits, like having the king in Wizard of Id make affectionate, love-filled comments about his subjects, or the mom in Baby Blues declare she loves temper tantrums.

In the minilesson on character continuity, I show two or three comic protagonists "staying in character" across several strips. The students and I discuss the characters' personality traits, interests, and concerns and examine the language the authors use to establish and maintain Garfield's gluttony, The Fusco Brothers' "loser" reputations, or Cathy's obsession with weight loss.

3. Transfer the learning to other writing. The cohesion-coherence making skills students develop in Missing Panels can be applied to and then reinforced and expanded in other genres of writing, for example, in journal entries, business letters, biographies, or social studies essays. Application of those skills, however, is not always automatic. Some students may believe that the sense-making conventions they learn in a comics activity are for comics only, unaware that many of the same elements that go into a Eudora Welty story or a Gabriel García Marquez novel also go into an Alley Oop, Momma, or For Better or For Worse strip. Students often need the teacher to pointedly suggest the transfer of skills, as in:

Remember when we looked at formal and informal language in our comics and talked about when it's smart to use one or the other? Use what you learned in the comics as you write your letters to the City Council about the new park plan.

Adopt-A-Strip

Materials: comic strips

Description: Students "adopt" favorite strips, read them daily, and periodically report to the class on plot developments.

Topics and Strategies:
- stand-alones versus continuity strips
- importance of student choice
- pair/small-group work
- increasing L2 input (reading)
- modeling (teacher adopting a strip)
- plot development reports
- text-to-text connections

Background

Newspaper comics (or the dailies) come in two basic types: stand-alones and continuity strips. Most are stand-alones, the one-shot gag strips. With stand-alones, a reader can easily—assuming enough L2—make sense of Wednesday's Wizard of Id, Lola, or The Piranha Club without having read Monday and Tuesday's strips. Familiarity with stock characters and running gags like Lucy's "holding" the football for Charlie Brown in Peanuts or Al's disaster dates in The Fusco Brothers enhance the humor, but stand-alone strips are comprehensible and funny without that background knowledge.

Continuity (or serialized) strips, like Brenda Starr, Gil Thorp, and Tarzan, on the other hand, spread a story over several installments, with some story arcs taking several weeks to complete. A reader can begin a continuity strip in the middle of a story arc and gradually catch up, but these strips, especially for second language learners, are best read from the beginning.

Process

Both types of comic will work for Adopt-A-Strip, but I strongly recommend that students go with a continuity strip whenever possible. (Please see Chapter 4 for a list of continuity strips available on the Web.) These strips, with their extended story lines, contain a full range of narrative material for discussion, including multiple conflicts, character development, and plot twists. They also provide more plot review and repetition of key story vocabulary, which aids comprehension and language development. Finally, they feature an element guaranteed to spur more second language reading: the daily cliff-hanger.

Regardless of the many advantages of the continuity strip, some students will want to adopt a one-shot like Agnes, Soup to Nutz, or Pooch Café. As strips go up for adoption, you're sure to hear something like: "If I don't adopt Spot the Frog I'll DIE!" And not necessarily from a second or third grader. The student could just as easily be a forty-five-year-old immigrant from El Salvador in your adult ed ESL conversation class who loves frogs, loves a frog named "Spot" in particular, and already considers the strip "her strip."

One of the quickest ways to kill the enjoyment and hence the effectiveness of this activity is to assign strips. I may gently try to nudge students away from the one-shots and toward the continuity strips, but I never force the issue. Students adopt a favorite strip—their favorite strip, not a strip I think should be one of their favorites. Adopting a stand-alone is hardly the end of the world. Students can still share some of the jokes and talk and write about Garfield's perennial laziness or the shameless audacity of Agnes. Also, some one-shot strips occasionally break the joke-a-day mold and include a story that stretches over a number of days, giving students a little more to discuss.

Several students, of course, may want to adopt the same strip; Duncan in a second-grade class, for example, or Baldo (see Figure 3–9) in a high school ELD (English Language Development) class. Pair or small-group adoption has some advantages: students can assist one another with the reading and always have someone at hand to discuss the latest story developments. Students can also prepare and present plot reports together, pooling language resources and at the same time, avoiding the anxiety many L2 learners feel when asked to produce oral or written material alone.

If you're wanting more "single student" adoptions and a wider range of strips read and discussed, consider a preliminary activity where you (and/or students) bring in a couple dozen different strips from local papers and comics websites. Rotate the strips around the room for all to read, then enourage students to branch out, leave their old favorites behind, and take a chance on a new comic. You may still have a couple diehard Herb & Jamaal or Grand Avenue fans who won't move beyond their pet strips, but most students will try a new comic if offered good alternatives. It also helps to remind students that adopting a new strip doesn't mean they're abandoning the old favorites. Though students

FIG. 3–9 Baldo *by Hector Cantú and Carlos Castellanos. Copyright © 2000 Baldo Partnership. Distributed by Universal Press Syndicate. Reprinted with permission. All rights reserved.*

report on the new strip, the old comics are read right along with the new. In the process, students increase L2 input.

Teachers may also want to adopt a new strip themselves as a vehicle for report modeling, for the sheer fun of it, and to prove to themselves that there really is a comics life after Calvin and Hobbes. Calvin's struggles with his long-suffering teacher, Miss Wormwood, made the strip a favorite with many educators. When Bill Watterson stopped drawing the strip in 1995, some of us went into comics-withdrawal. Fortunately, books of Calvin and Hobbes reprints are still available. 'Ninety-five, by the way, was a tough year for comics readers. We also lost Gary Larson's The Far Side and Berkeley Breathed's Outland (with Opus, the penguin). Had Peanuts ended the same year, I may never have opened another newspaper again in my life.

Plot development reports can be oral or written and scheduled as often as student interest and time permit. Some classes do updates once a week, others once a month. After a while, students become resident experts on a strip, using notes made during their comics reading to summarize and update classmates on the latest happenings in Pickles or Preteena. Apart from the updates, you'll typically hear students make text-to-text connections, using characters from their adopted comic to discuss—and better understand—the motivations and actions of characters in other non-comic reading.

Funny or Not?

Materials: cartoons and comic strips

Description: Students work in pairs or small groups, figuring out the jokes in comics and rating them on a humor scale.

Topics and Strategies:
- wordplay in humor
- culturally bound humor
- using mixed language proficiency groups
- making text-to-self connections
- difficulty of "outside" jokes
- importance of teachers trying activity themselves
- learning language, learning culture

Background

Jokes are tough in a second language. The humor in comics ofen hinges on a single word. Miss that key word and you miss the joke. Worse, students may know the key word and still miss the joke, since wordplay typically relies on alternate meanings to generate the laugh. Students operating with only one definition for "stable" or "pitch" will find the two Grimmy strips (Figures 3–10 and 3–11) incomprehensible.

It gets tougher. Besides the frequent wordplay, jokes are culturally bound. Miss or misunderstand a key cultural reference or an aspect of the cultural backdrop in a comic and again, you miss the joke. The Monkey Business strip (Figure 3–12) may be a "head shaker" to students unfamiliar with actor Brad Pitt or baffled by a cultural norm that permits girls to comment on a boy's physical appearance. Even "bolder" comments appear in Figure 3–13. And without knowing the slang term "wedgie," the strip is over for a student before it begins. Culture-bound comics are demanding reads, even for those students with intermediate to advanced L2 proficiency who may know the meanings—and multiple meanings—of hundreds and hundreds of content words. I remember one intermediate-level fourth grader struggling with a Citizen Dog strip and declaring, "I know all words! All! But what is mean, Teacher?!" She knew the words, but not the culture.

FIG. 3–10 *Grimmy by Mike Peters. Copyright © 1999 by Grimmy, Inc. Reprinted with special permission of King Features Sydndicate.*

FIG. 3–11 *Grimmy by Mike Peters. Copyright © 1999 by Grimmy, Inc. Reprinted with special permission of King Features Sydndicate.*

FIG. 3–12 Monkey Business *by Karl Wang. Copyright © 2004 by Karl Wang. Reprinted by permission of the author,* <www.monkey-business.net/>.

Let's take a Shirley & Son strip (Figure 3–14) as an example. The strip will mean little if, one, you don't know what a toaster is and, two, you've never heard of that all-American snack favorite, the "poptart." In addition to the two explicit references (one visual, one verbal), readers must also understand the strip's implicit information, including the fact that lots of American kids:

- must fix their own breakfast and snacks;
- eat on the run;
- and rarely use any appliance other than a microwave.

Without those implicit, "under the surface" items, the comic won't be fully comprehensible or funny.

Process

After modeling the basic process at the overhead with a sample comic or two, I set students off to work. Whenever possible, I use mixed language proficiency groupings so that beginners always have help at hand. Three questions guide student work:

1. What does the comic SAY? Students decode the cartoon or strip, no easy feat for L2 beginners dealing with a new set of sound-symbol relationships.

2. What does the comic MEAN? Students discuss alternate meanings (this phrase means . . . , but it could also mean . . .), pinpoint trouble spots (What does the boy mean here . . . ?), and use their prior knowledge combined with visual and text clues to understand the comic.

FIG. 3–13 Mr. & Mrs. Smarty Pants *by Penny Van Horn. Copyright © 1998 by Penny Van Horn. Reprinted by permission of the author,* <www.pennyvanhorn.com/>.

3. Is the comic FUNNY? Students make judgment calls on the comic's humor. Lower-grade students rate the comic as: not funny!, funny, or really funny! Upper elementary, secondary, and adult learners use a point scale, running from 1(a total loser!) to a high of 5 (made me laugh out loud!). Three students in Beverly Williams' sixth-grade class in Daly City, California, made widely differing calls on the Baby Blues strip in Figure 3–15. Alaa Hammoudeh gave it a 1 because something in the strip did not ring true. He asked, "How can you see her loose tooth is nasty?" in his comic response log. Classmate Michelle Pimentel, on

FIG. 3–14 Shirley & Son *by Jerry Bittle. Copyright © 2002 by Jerry Bittle. Reprinted by permission of United Feature Syndicate, Inc.*

FIG. 3–15 Baby Blues *by Jerry Scott and Rick Kirkman. Copyright © 2001 by Jerry Scott and Rick Kirkman. Reprinted by special permission of King Features Syndicate.*

the other hand, thought the comic was a winner. She gave it a 5 and commented that "The crying baby boy in the cartoon is like my little brother always borther [bother] me." Katia Lopez took the middle ground and rated the strip a 3. She explained that ". . . everytime when I get a loose tooth I look the mirror and I think it's gross. I gross myself." Evidently "gross" was a little funny, but not funny in the exteme.

I often have pairs make collective judgment calls. Having small groups reach consensus on whether that Soup to Nutz strip was a washout or a winner will generate lots of great cross-talk, but may take the entire school day. And some groups won't be able to agree on a rating given a year. As an alternative, I ask each person in the group to rate the comic. Numbers are then averaged to determine the group rating. A companion question to number 3 is always: What makes the comic funny? Or not funny? As students rate comics and present their "funny reports" to the class, they return to the text (written and visual) for evidence to substantiate their ratings. Requiring evidence creates the need to read and reread carefully and critically.

Throughout the activity, students are encouraged to connect happenings and emotions in the comics to their own experiences. Lots of humor is universal. Regardless of the cultural makeup of your classroom, most students will be laughing at the same jokes. But not everyone. A joke or anecdote is often funny because we see ourselves reflected in it; our laugh is the laugh of recognition. Humor that lies outside our realm of experience is not as easily recognized. "Outside" jokes may be seen as odd and humorless, or in comics with several culture-specific references, not seen at all. Some jokes will fly right past some students. Second language learners, especially beginners, may rate these "outside" jokes considerably lower on the funny scale than their more L2-proficient and native-speaking peers.

Make sure you've got a good pair of walking shoes for this activity. Running shoes might be even better, since you'll be racing from group to group, trying to get to everybody dying to share ratings with you. Students will also want to know how you rate the comics. Is that Loose Parts cartoon funny? Or *really* funny? Beyond asking for your opinion—and your evidence for that opinion— students will have dozens and dozens of questions related to comic content. Even in a class with mostly intermediate to advanced L2 learners, you'll be regularly asked to mediate, to clarify the written and visual text information in the comics—to help students get the jokes.

One of the best ways to understand the challenge facing your students with Funny or Not? is to try the activity yourself in your second language. If you're at an intermediate or early advanced level in L2, you'll be surprised at how many comprehension snags there can be, as a teacher who tried the activity in Spanish told me, "in one little bitty comic."

Interactive Journals

Materials: cartoons and comic strips

Description: Students and teacher trade journal entries regarding favorite comics.

Topics and Strategies:
- authentic writing
- message over form
- improving vocabulary, mechanics, grammar
- writing from outside and inside the comic
- teacher journals
- teacher journal overload
- buddy journals
- online journaling

Background

Interactive journals are popular and effective vehicles for stimulating L2 writing (Peyton and Reed 1990; Peyton and Staton 1996). Though seen most often in the elementary grades, the journals can be used with equally positive results by secondary and adult education teachers. Their popularity and effectiveness hinge on the authentic nature of the writing. In interactive journals, students and teacher exchange questions, comments, ideas, jokes, and anecdotes about topics of mutual interest. The journal entries are voluntary and ungraded, with the teacher focusing on message over form, on what students are saying rather than on how they're saying it.

Though the result may appear counterintuitive to teachers new to the process, taking the spotlight off form can actually help improve it. Students freed from the mandate to "write right," to get everything correct, typically write more and risk more with language, two key ingredients in becoming a better writer. The motivation to communicate is high with interactive journals and students work hard at making sure their entries are understandable. Making them understandable, in turn, requires attention to L2 conventions, to mechanics (spelling, punctuation, capitalization) and grammar—for example, to pronoun-antecedent agreement, tense choice, comparison of adjectives and adverbs, and the use of subordinating conjunctions.

Process

In this activity, students snip favorite cartoons and comic strips out of magazines and newspapers and paste or tape them into their journals as a base for dialogue with the teacher. Students who are big comics fans might add a new comic once or twice a week; less enthusiastic fans perhaps once a month. The raw material for increasing vocabulary, cleaning up nonstandard spellings, or learning irregular verb forms may come from the language in the comics pasted into the journal or from the language in the teacher's entries.

Journal entries are customarily done with an omniscient viewpoint, with student and teacher standing outside the comic looking in, making observations, posing questions about plot development, commenting on the humor and language, and relating aspects of the comic to their own lives. A less common, but for some students a more interesting and liberating route, is to write from inside the comic, making comments from the point of view of one of the characters, say as Bucky Katt in Get Fuzzy or as Helen in Helen, Sweetheart of the Internet. The teacher responds in the voice of a different character. By the way, if your favorite comics aren't appearing in student journals, there's an easy fix: Snip and paste the favorites into your own journal and let it periodically circulate through the room for comment and questions.

> ### Field Sketch: A Journal Winner
>
> I love using comics. My favorites are Calvin and Hobbes and Garfield. What I do is white out the dialogue and make copies for my students to paste into their writing journals. They make up their own stories. We read the different versions aloud. It is their favorite type of journal entry. My students are sixth to eighth graders from Eastern Europe and India.
>
> —Corrien Mateo, ESL teacher
> Joliet, Illinois

Understandably, some teachers steer clear of interactive journals because of the work involved. Responding to student entries with anything more than an "I agree!" or "What will Heathcliff do?" is a tiring, time-consuming business. As a young teacher more years ago than I care to remember, I began interactive journals by responding to all twenty-two student journals three times a week. By the end of a month, I was on overload and ready to call it quits on this type of journaling. The only way I kept the journals going was by dramatically scaling back, responding to half the journals once a week and the other half the next.

Beyond a basic cutback, the obvious solution to journal overload is to move to buddy journals where students exchange entries with other students. Many teachers do a combination of student-teacher and student-student journals. Comics-based buddy journals work especially well online. Students can choose from hundreds of different cartoons and strips available on the Web, download a favorite, compose an entry, and email it to their journal buddy for reaction. Please see Chapter 4 for Web addresses of major comics sites.

Word Study

Materials: comic strips

Description: Students use comics as a base for word study.

Topics and Strategies:
- relevancy and context for word study
- word study targets
- keeping the focus on the comic

Background

All teachers with second language learners work to some extent on the basic building blocks of language: words. In content classes at the secondary level, the work is typically infrequent, unplanned, and brief. An American history teacher may take a moment to explain the prefixes *anti* and *pro* in relation to gun control issues; an algebra teacher may point out synonyms (rate, pace, speed, velocity) to help students make sense of motion problems.

In self-contained classrooms in the lower grades and in second language classes at all levels, word work, commonly called word study or language and word study (Fountas and Pinnell 2001), is often a core program component, done daily and carefully structured. A fourth-grade teacher, for example, may open her morning language arts block with a half-hour word study followed by an hour reading workshop and an hour writing workshop. An adult ed ESL teacher may include a ten- to fifteen-minute word study with nearly every reading selection. During word study time, teachers offer explicit instruction and guided practice on recognizing, decoding, comprehending, spelling, and appropriately using words in the new language.

Word studies with second language learners can be tricky and not always as effective as we'd like. To illustrate the point, let's imagine we're off to Mexico this summer and before heading south, we enroll in a community college Spanish class to improve our language skills. We're about a 2 on a 5-point scale, early intermediate level at best. Our instructor does a word study with us each session. Today we spend forty minutes developing a semantic field (word family) of writing and drawing instruments. Our chart paper lists the following: *lápiz, lápiz de color, lápiz mecánico, marcador, bolígrafo, pluma, colores,* and *pinceles.* We consider sound-letter correspondences, roots, affixes, look for spelling patterns, do a quick word sort (accented versus nonaccented), and discuss which words work where, for example, artists use *pinceles* (brushes) and architects use *lápices mecánicos* (mechanical pencils).

Along the way, we build a number of phonics, word recognition, spelling, and usage skills. We add to the stockpile of our Spanish vocabulary. Or perhaps not. If we perceive the targeted items as irrelevant (we want to eat in Mexico, not paint or draw up house plans!), or if the items are never sufficiently contextualized with objects, visuals, or movement to make them comprehensible, we pick up few skills.

As adults, of course, we can drop a dull, ineffective class. Most students don't have that option. About a year ago, I watched a group of third-grade English language beginners do a word sort with verbs, nouns, and adjectives, pulled from a commercial, publisher-provided list and written on three-by-five-inch cards. As they worked, I joined the group and casually asked what the words meant. Together, they knew two or three, but the vast majority of the words were total mysteries. Nevertheless, the students dutifully sorted, essentially sorting to sort.

Without relevancy and context, word studies offer second language learners little more than the illusion of learning. Make them relevant and contextualized, however, and it's a new instructional ball game. If we switch to food items and restaurant menus in our Spanish-for-teachers example, and pull words from an exciting, picture-heavy read-aloud for our third graders, word studies provide considerable language learning opportunities.

Comics are an ideal vehicle for word study. First, their pop culture topics, offbeat characters, humor, and adventure make them relevant. Most students find comics inherently fun and interesting. Second, their pictures offer context clues that help make written text and, hence, the words for word study understandable. For many students, the same text would be unintelligible if found in pictureless material—for example, in a short story, novel, or email. Third, the reduced text in comics lightens the language-processing load for L2 learners. Teacher and students still have plenty of challenging text for word studies, but conduct those studies with a more manageable amount of text.

Process

Here's one possible format for doing word studies with comics.

Step One: Target

The teacher chooses the target or objective for the word study based on student language needs. Needs are pinpointed through both formal and informal assessment. Formal assessment might include district- or state-mandated language proficiency tests, standardized achievement tests, and teacher-designed subject quizzes and tests. Informal assesment might include student oral interviews and observations, and reviews of written products like journals, stories, poems, letters, and reports.

Study targets involve an area of mechanics (spelling, punctuation, and capitalization) or any of the language subsystems.

Subsystem	Examples
phonology (sounds)	• intonation patterns • word stress • digraphs (ch, ph, gh) • phonemes (/v/ versus /b/)
morphology (word construction)	• regular versus irregular past tense • comparatives (high, higher, highest) • compound words • plurals (-s versus -es versus -ies) • affixes (prefixes, suffixes)
syntax (sentence construction)	• subject-verb-object pattern • combining ideas with conjunctions • indirect object placement • separable verbs (give up, spread out)
lexicon (vocabulary) and semantics (meaning)	• word choice • collocations (birthday and present) • idioms and colloquialisms • homophones and homographs • cognates and false cognates
pragmatics (language in context)	• gambits (conversation openings) • register (informal versus formal forms) • implications • body language

The chart above provides only a small sampling of potential targets. We'll always have more targets than time. So which targets warrant a study? One rule of thumb: When ongoing assessment locates an element posing problems for a third or more of your students, it qualifies for a word study.

Step Two: Minilesson

The teacher does a minilesson at the overhead (or with a computer projector) using cartoons and comic strips that show the selected language target or targets. See Figure 3–16 for a comic used with high schoolers to discuss gambits and question structures. Building up a stock of comics containing the elements you need takes time. But once you've got your antenna up, meaning you read the daily comics page with a cup of coffee in one hand and scissors in the other, you'll find lots of usable strips. When I locate another "just right" comic, I snip, make a transparency, write up a few teaching notes if needed, stick everything in a folder, and label. If you need to keep your newspapers and magazines pristine and whole, snip electronically from the Web.

Minilessons are tightly focused and short. Depending on grade level and number of targets, a minilesson might run from ten to twenty minutes. Though minilessons are generally done with the whole class, they don't have to be. In other comics-based activities, I sometimes do spur-of-the-moment, ad hoc word studies with one or more students as I move group to group during guided practice.

Regardless of where and when word studies are done, it's important to remember that what students are chiefly interested in is the comic, not the element of word study within the comic. Once we've highlighted the target element and discussed how that element works to help us (1) make sense of the comic and (2) communicate more effectively in our second language in a given setting, the direct instruction portion of the word study ends. If it doesn't, we run the risk of explaining mechanics and grammar to explain mechanics and grammar. We may lose student interest, kill the enjoyment in the comic, and disconnect word study from real-world communication.

For example, imagine using Jordan Crane's Col Dee (Figure 3–17) to target tense shift in narrative writing. We pinpoint verbs, explain, ask for questions, pinpoint some more verbs, then explain everything again for good measure. After all the pinpointing and explaining, there's little time left for discussing the comic's core themes of single parenting, unemployment, honesty, and caring for a dying pet. My guideline: never sacrifice a good story for a word study.

> ### Field Sketch: Looking for Idioms
>
> After reading the graphic novel, *INUYASHA*: I would like to read it again! I like to discover idioms and the way that American use their words. [unedited comments]
>
> —Uyen Thai, Student
> Chuck Kaspar, Instructor
> Intermediate/Adv. ESL Adult Education Class
> Independence Adult Center
> San Jose, California

Step Three: Application

Students apply what they've learned in word study to other classroom work. Sometimes the work immediately follows the study as guided practice. For example, students might be asked to read several strips zeroing in on contracted forms (I'm, she's, they'd, you'd, he'll, we'll) to help them know when characters are talking about the present, past, or future—just as the teacher had modeled in the word study.

At other times, students use knowledge picked up in comics-based word studies and apply it to non-comics work. For example, if our word studies have targeted cognates, metaphors, and conversation close signals, you might see

FIG. 3–16 *"The Butterfingered Offing"* by Samuel Kienbaum and Chris Kohler originally published in Garish Zow Comics (no. 5). Copyright © 2004 by Samuel Kienbaum and Chris Kohler. Reprinted by permission of Hidden Agenda Press, <www.hiddenagendapress.com/>.

FIG. 3–17 *From Col Dee by Jordan Crane. Copyright © 2001 by Jordan Crane. Reprinted by permission of Reddingk,* <www.reddingk.com/>.

students using cognates to increase their understanding of a passage in the social studies text, including more metaphors in their original poems, and ending an intergroup discussion of physics experiments with, "Well, that's all the data we have."

One last plug for using comics for word study. Most teachers working with second language learners have students at various proficiency stages. Many, especially resource, community college, and adult ed teachers, also have students who differ widely in age, life experience, and language goals. Given that huge range of need, teachers naturally gravitate to activities and materials that will work for lots of different students, not just a few. Enter comics. About a month ago, in the span of two weeks, I did some language and word study work with second graders (capitals and question marks), sixth graders (homophones), high schoolers (informal versus formal register), and graduate students at the University of San Francisco (cohesive ties, prosody, and speech acts). In all the settings, I used comics—the same comics. Peanuts had something for everybody. A tip of the hat to Charles Schulz!

Panel Detectives

Materials: newspaper comics

Description: Students investigate a wide range of issues in local newspaper comics.

Topics and Strategies:
- language hypothesizing
- risking with language
- high-interest curriculum
- comics as vehicles for social research

Background

Language acquisition is a trial-and-error process. As students move down the developmental highway in any language, first or second, they form hypotheses about how the language works. For example, a third-grade L2 beginner may decide that the past tense of "eat" must be "eated" because so many other verbs in English work like that. Add an -ed to any verb and you can instantly talk about what happened yesterday or a year ago. The student then tests out the newly minted form with teacher, classmates, and neighborhood friends, and keeps or discards the form based on the feedback she receives.

If the form consistently advances conversation, the hypothesis is validated. The form is a keeper. If the form consistently impedes conversation, the hypothesis is invalidated; "eated" is a loser and discarded. In this case, a more communicative form would be "ate," a construction our third grader hears frequently when she tests "eated." For example:

STUDENT: I eated early.
TEACHER: What?
STUDENT: I eated lunch early.
TEACHER: Oh, you ate early. Me too.

After a few tryouts like this, the student commonly swaps the problematic "eated" for the more workable "ate." This trial-and-error process, so critical for language acquisition (Brown 2000), hinges on a student's willingness to risk—to make mistakes. Students are much more likely to risk in a classroom where they feel psychologically safe, where teacher and peers see their errors as a natural part of the second language landscape. In such a classroom, students feel free to get language wrong on their way to getting it right. Errors are certainly still dealt with and cleaned up, either indirectly through modeling as in the example above, or directly through targeted instruction and guided practice, but always with a focus on communication.

A nonthreatening, communicative-based classroom is a necessary condition for language acquisition, but not a sufficient one. Equally important is a high-interest curriculum. Without something engaging to talk about, why talk? You'll get plenty of talk with Panel Detectives. In fact, once students begin sharing what they discover in this activity, it's hard to get them to stop the talk, a problem most language teachers would love to have!

Process

Students work in small groups using comics from the local paper as raw material for their research. Each detective team investigates a specific issue framed as a question. The issues, depending on grade level and student interests, run the gamut from gender roles, language use, and ethnic diversity, to stereotyping, ageism, and relationship conflicts. Possible questions include:

1. How many strips are drawn by women?
2. How many characters are male?
3. What jobs do men and women have?
4. What themes appear in strips drawn by women? by men?
5. How many strips feature children as main characters?
6. How many strips feature child-parent conflicts?
7. What is the average age of male characters? female? child?
8. How many strips feature African Americans (Latinos, Asians, Native Americans, etc.)?

9. How many strips feature a sports (school, family, dating, military, historical, etc.) setting?
10. How many violent versus altruistic acts occur in the strips?
11. Who uses more slang in the strips, men or women? adults or kids?
12. What stereotypes appear in the strips?
13. What animals are portrayed as smart? as dumb?
14. How many strips deal with relationship problems?
15. How many strips incorporate current events?
16. How many strips feature idioms? colloquialisms? dialect?
17. How many strips deal with religion? sexual orientation?
18. How many joke strips show teasing? slapstick? wordplay?
19. How many strips feature adult themes? child themes?
20. What are the most common professions shown in strips?

Though a single page of comics may provide some insights, for example, that only three out of twenty strips in the San Francisco Chronicle (at this writing) are drawn by women—most questions will require a week to several weeks of strips to answer with any authority. If you're fortunate enough to live in a city that supports more than one newspaper, students will have more comics to research and can compare and contrast findings across papers. You'll also find hundreds of comics online, enough for the most ambitious group of panel detectives. See Chapter 4 for website suggestions. Finally, some of your second language learners may want to do additional detective work with strips in non-English papers and on non-English comics websites. This opens the door to a wealth of intriguing—and talk-inducing!—cross-cultural comparisons and contrasts.

Once the comics pages are pulled from the paper or located online, groups follow a five-step process.

Step One: Question
Groups choose their research question from a list generated by the class in a teacher-led discussion. Each group researches a different question.

Step Two: Hypothesis
Before beginning any detective work, students make a hypothesis, their best guess to answer the research question. If the question is "How many strips show men doing domestic chores or taking care of kids?" the hypothesis might be: 15 percent of the strips in four weeks of the New York Times will show men doing domestic chores or taking care of kids.

Step Three: Research
Students check all strips on the comics pages and record target data. For example, if the group wants to answer the question, "How many strips with children and adults show the children as troublemakers?" students record the total number of strips with children and adults and tally each instance of troublemaking by

Men's Jobs		Women's Jobs
• police officer	• ball player	• sales clerk
• custodian	• announcer	• housewife
• chef	• auditor	• auditor
• student	• clown	• nurse
• teacher	• driver	• librarian
• warrior	• executive	

Social and Family Issues

• fighting	• family (arguing)
• killing	• family (screaming)
• men tired of war	• family (snoring)
• terrorism	• older men hating young men
• men making jokes about women	• teaching children to behave
• worrying about losing a job	• smoking
• not communicating	• drugs
• car accidents	

Data from Advanced ELD group, Santa Clara High School, Santa Clara, California, Jeff Zwiers, teacher. Results are based on two weeks' worth of comic strips from the San Francisco Chronicle, fall 2003. Each item listed was tallied at least once.

FIG. 3–18: *Panel Detective Data*

a child or an adult. Some research questions can be answered quickly, for example, "How many strips feature Chinese American characters?" Others require much more time, as in "Who uses more slang, adults or kids?" If groups are to work the same amount of time on the activity, say three fifty-minute sessions, those with quick-answer questions may need one or more backup questions to stay engaged.

See Figure 3–18 for research data from a group of high school second language learners in Santa Clara, California, who posed two questions: (1) What type of jobs do men and women do in the comics? and (2) What type of social/family issues do comics talk about?

Step Four: Data Analysis and Answer

Students analyze their data, convert tally totals to percentages when appropriate, and answer their original question or questions. One group of third graders in the San Francisco Bay Area asked, "How many strips in the local paper feature Latino characters?" Their answer: ZERO! Three of the four kids in the group were of Mexican heritage.

Step Five: Report

Each group reports its findings to the class with tallies and totals displayed on overhead transparencies, chart paper, or poster board. Passions run high when groups gather data on issues related to gender, ethnicity, and stereotyping, and discussions are lively. Students are quick to share reactions and opinions regarding what they found while working as comics detectives. You may see students who rarely speak in front of the class freely risking in their second language, commenting on results they found surprising or blatantly discriminatory.

Reports don't have to remain in-house. Some groups like to share their findings with the editor of the local comics page or with the content manager of a comics site. Though these letters and email sometimes applaud editors and managers for including a particular strip, more frequently they take the powers that be to task for their paper or site's woeful lack of diversity.

Take-A-Stand

Materials: editorial cartoons

Description: Students analyze editorial cartoons and use them as models to create their own cartoons on personal, school, and local community issues.

Topics and Strategies:
- editorial cartoons
- cartoons for critical thinking
- critical literacy approach

Background

In teacher workshops and university classes on second language issues, I always pose the "do" question: What do your students need to *do* with English? Responses typically echo district and state English Language Development standards:

- answer simple questions with one- or two-word responses
- prepare and deliver short oral presentations
- identify specific facts in expository text
- analyze rhetorical styles in consumer materials
- create cohesive paragraphs that develop a central idea
- prepare clear business letters, job applications, resumes

Often the "dos" are stated in less formal terms:

- carry on a conversation
- tell stories

- read a newspaper
- be a smart shopper
- write an essay
- get and keep a job

In a quarter hour, teachers easily generate a list of forty or more items. I can never write fast enough at the overhead or on chart paper to record everybody's "dos." Inevitably, as we scrutinize the list and discuss the language skills needed for meeting particular standards, someone will mention the fact that critical thinking underpins most if not all the items. Students can't do much with English unless they can classify, organize, inference, summarize, synthesize, and evaluate. Once we agree on the need to build critical thinking skills as we build language skills and content knowledge, it's a short hop to critical literacy.

A critical literacy approach (Freire 1970; Ada 1988; Wink 2000) emphasizes text analysis, personal reflection, and social action. Students read with critical eyes, examining the text for surface (explicit) and subsurface (implicit) messages related to a variety of social justice issues, including stereotyping; discrimination; racism; and gender, sexual orientation, and language bias. With the teacher guiding and mediating when necessary, students reflect on similar issues in their own lives, comparing and contrasting their experiences with those of other people in various books and articles. Some students may be critically reflecting in their first language, some in both first and second. Students with beginning second language skills may need to bridge to their teacher and classmates through a bilingual buddy, cross-age tutor, instructional aide, or parent volunteer.

Finally, students choose issues for social action. Depending on grade level and issue, actions might include one or more of the following: writing elected representatives, creating and performing a puppet play for other classes, establishing an informational website, publishing a newsletter, launching a petition drive, or organizing a boycott.

Process

Take-A-Stand provides another social action option: creating and publishing editorial cartoons. At the start, students gather cartoons from newspapers, magazines, and various comics sites on the Web. (See Chapter 4 for editorial cartoon websites, and Figures 3–19 and 3–20 for some great cartoons by Penny Van Horn.) Each student brings one or two comics to class related to issues of personal interest. After some teacher modeling at the overhead, students share their comics in pairs or small groups and try their best to make sense of all visual and written text. Try, but not necessarily succeed. Students quickly realize that understanding editorial cartoons, even identifying the central issue in a cartoon, can be a struggle. Merely figuring out the literal meaning of the comic's few words takes considerable work for many second language learners.

Even with the words deciphered, the comic may remain incomprehensible. Editorial cartoons are topical. They spring from the latest events, people, and

FIG. 3–19 Modern Taunts *by Penny Van Horn. Copyright © 2000 by Penny Van Horn. Reprinted by permission of the author,* <www.pennyvanhorn.com/>.

issues in the news. If you follow the news you get the joke; if you don't, you miss it. Obviously, native speakers will have far fewer problems with basic text comprehension than their L2 learner peers. Getting the jokes as a native speaker, however, may prove just as difficult. Students who can't name the governor of their own state or believe the phrase "energy crisis" only refers to ballplayers in

FIG. 3–20 Explaining Obesity in America *by Penny Van Horn. Copyright © 2002 by Penny Van Horn. Reprinted by permission of the author,* <www.pennyvanhorn.com/>.

a slump will be at a loss with most editorial cartoons—regardless of English proficiency level. Those students might be fourth graders but could just as easily be news-oblivious high school juniors or seniors. If students get interested in editorial cartoons and the activity is repeated several times over a few weeks or months, you'll see more students following the news, if not in newspapers or magazines, at least on radio or TV.

Once students have made sense of the cartoons, teased out and discussed key social issues, and connected the issues to their personal lives, they take on a single problem, as one L2 middle schooler enthusiastically put it, "for big action!" A class of thirty students might work in small groups on several different issues. Dorothy Burt's second language learners at Ygnacio Valley High in Concord, California, targeted the homeless, the war in Iraq, and banned soda sales (see Figures 3–21, 3–22, and 3–23). Terrible school food—watch out for the beef ribs!—and inadequate classroom electrical outlets spurred Beverly Williams' sixth graders to action at Westlake School in Daly City, California (see Figures 3–24 and 3–25). Some issues, however, may resonate with an entire class: racial epithets used in school hallways, gender inequity in a district's sport programs, or employment discrimination or library censorship in the local community. When this happens, all students work on the same issue or on different aspects of the same issue in small groups.

Students create individual cartoons, but assist one another throughout the production cycle of drafting, feedback, revision, and publication. As they work, students use the cartoons posted around the room or those they've collected in notebooks as models. The professional comics provide hints on editorial cartoon conventions; for example, minimal text, exaggerated physical features, and a pointed message that skewers the political opposition. Students can also turn to the cartoon models for key vocabulary associated with particular social issues.

Consistent with a critical literacy approach, students learn that real editorial cartoonists have real readers, all potential allies for solving specific social problems. Finding those readers means that simply publishing the cartoons for the teacher or classmates isn't enough—not for social action. Students decide where to publish their cartoons based on where they'll get read and where they'll have the most impact. Depending on the interest level of the issue—local, regional, national, or international—cartoons are published (or posted) in one or more places, including school newspapers and newsletters, city newspapers, school and student websites, city halls, stores, and mall displays. Some students send their editorial cartoons with a cover letter to select business and government officials.

Take-A-Stand levels the playing field for beginning second language learners. Because of the predominance of visual material in editorial cartoons, beginners—with only a few words of text—can create comics that are just as insightful, communicative, and effective as a social action message as their more advanced L2 classmates.

FIG. 3–21 *Homeless. Ayesha Achakzai, grade 11, Ygnacio Valley High School, Concord, California.*

To facilitate discussion of the cartoons and as an aid to looking at their political content, I sometimes ask students to tape a commercial or student-made cartoon to a long chalk line I've drawn on the blackboard and labeled LEFT . . . CENTER . . . RIGHT. Some of the richest discussions I've had with Take-A-Stand (for both language and history/social science content learning) have come from the placement of a cartoon either too close to or too far away from the political center.

FIG. 3–22 *Iraq. Sara Jeilli Bargzie, grade 11, Ygnacio Valley High School, Concord, California.*

FIG. 3–23 *Banned Soda. Jian Ou, grade 11, Ygnacio Valley High School, Concord, California.*

FIG. 3–24 *Gross Food. Mandy Chew, grade 6, Westlake School, Daly City, California.*

FIG. 3–25 *No Power. Gus Hernandez, grade 6, Westlake School, Daly City, California.*

Time Traveler

Materials: comic books

Description: Students research social issues using comic books from various eras.

Topics and Strategies:
- comics as research materials
- social issue change across time
- lively talk for language development
- vintage comics reprints

Background

A number of the early comic book action heroes and superheroes (action heroes with unearthly powers) are still going strong. Superman (1938), Batman (1939), The Flash (1940), and Wonder Woman (1941), for example, continue their fight against the forces of evil and injustice everywhere. And unlike the rest of us mere mortals whose middles expand and tops thin with time, these guys (and gal) are looking good. In fact, most look better than they did over a half century ago. Many of the villains and supervillains, the characters comics fans love to hate, have also been around for years: The Joker and Catwoman (in Batman, 1940), Lex Luthor (in Superman, 1941), Two-Face (in Detective Comics, 1942), and Cheetah (in Wonder Woman, 1943), are still bad to the bone, as irrepressibly and deliciously wicked as ever. And thank heavens, since without them, our heroes and superheroes wouldn't need to be nearly as heroic.

Yet despite the consistency of some characters and core elements—the superhuman powers, the skintight costumes, the dual identities, the mix of science fact and fiction, and our hero's one fatal flaw, green kryptonite for Superman and the bracelets of submission for Wonder Woman—superhero comics have changed on numerous fronts over the decades. So have other genres of comics. Both the similarities and differences across eras provide students with a mountain of interesting material for small-group research and discussion.

Process

In Time Traveler, students work in small groups with two sets of comic books. Set one contains recently published titles, set two has comics anywhere from two to six decades older. Students read comics from one era, then "time travel" to another via the second set. As they move back and forth between eras, students compare and contrast the comics in terms of one or more key elements, including:

- the big ideas (themes/issues), featured and ignored
- gender roles and relationships
- representation and treatment of minorities

- stereotyping and scapegoating
- type and amount of violence
- type of justice (vigilante versus court)
- hero's personality traits
- hero's physical characteristics
- type and use of technology
- background (clothing, hair styles, furnishings, vehicles)
- use of idioms, slang, colloquialisms, collocations
- artistic style and storytelling craft

Depending on the type of discussion you're after—wide-ranging or narrowly focused—each group can tackle a different element, or all groups can investigate the same element, say hero/heroine body shape or the depiction of scientists, teachers, or business owners.

How far back in time students travel and how many stops they make along the way also varies. One group may want to tally and compare the amount of violence used by the Dark Knight (Batman) in only two time zones, now and in the stories from the 1950s. Another group may want to race alongside The Scarlet Speedster (The Flash) through each decade beginning in the 1940s, contrasting the ethnicity of "bad guys" and "good guys." See Figure 3–26 for one of the contemporary comics used by an ESL adult class to probe thirty years of crime comics, zeroing in on "women's responses to attack."

I recently recommended Gene Luen Yang's "American Born Chinese" (Figure 3–27) to a group of middle schoolers investigating racial stereotypes. The group used Yang's webcomic, which deals with a variety of Chinese American issues including stereotyping and racism, as a starting point, then looked at portrayals of Chinese Amercians and other Asian Americans (when portrayed at all!) in several genres of comics back through the 1950s. A second group investigated gender roles and mother-daughter relationships using Robbins' and Timmons' current GoGirl! comics (Figure 3–28a & b) and several romance comics of the 1940s and 50s, with titles like Young Romance, In Love, My Romance, and Hi-School Romance.

Groups present their Time Traveler investigations orally or in writing. Oral reports generate lots of cross-talk—and vigorous debate. Be prepared to mediate, moderate, and just plain "keep the lid on" as students share findings and feelings related to sexism, racial discrimination, class warfare, crime and punishment, acculturation versus assimilation, and a host of superhero-mortal relationship issues. This is not a quiet activity; students talk up a storm, which is exactly what we want for language development. With little to no teacher encouragement, students typically broaden their investigations and discussions to include other non-comic material they're reading at school and at home.

Finally, a note on materials. Without a good selection of comics going back at least two decades (at a minimum), your time-traveling students may return to the present without the data they need to create strong, meaty reports. Two sets of Spider-Man comics a few years apart will differ only slightly on hero

FIG. 3–26 *"Perfect Pitch" by Tim Goodyear and Adam Stone originally published in* Garish Zow Comics *(no.2). Copyright © 2002 by Tim Goodyear and Adam Stone. Reprinted by permission of Hidden Agenda Press,* <www.hiddenagendapress.com/>.

traits, language, themes, and social issues. Increasing the time range between sets increases differences and gives students more material for comparing and contrasting key elements.

Fortunately, you can still buy lots of twenty- to thirty-year-old (non-collectible) comics for a song, usually twenty-five cents to a couple dollars a piece at your local comics shop. Older and collectible comics, though perfect for the Time Traveler activity, cost more. A lot more. Stick with the non-collectibles, or better yet, use reprints of the collectibles. Your local comics shop will have several volumes of reasonably priced vintage reprints. Also check your public library.

Here are some reprint winners: The Secret Origins Replica Edition (DC Comics, 1998) features late fifties–early sixties stories with some big-name superheroes, including Superman, Batman, Green Lantern, Wonder Woman, The Flash, and J'onn J'onzz, the Manhunter from Mars. The same heroes appear in DC's current Justice League of America comics. Heroes from the Marvel Comics Universe, including Spider-Man (Figure 3–29), X-Men, and Daredevil (Figure 3–30), can be found in Fantastic Firsts (Marvel Comics, 2002), a reprint

FIG. 3–27 *From* American Born Chinese: Book One *by Gene Yang. Copyright © 2002 by Gene Yang. Reprinted by permission of the author,* <www.geocities.com/misteryang/>.

FIG. 3–28a *From GoGirl! by Trina Robbins and Anne Timmons. Copyright © 2002 by Trina Robbins and Anne Timmons. Reprinted by permission of the authors; Trina Robbins (<www.popimage.com/gogirl/>), Anne Timmons (<homepage.mac.com/tafrin/>), Dark Horse Comics (<www.darkhorse.com/>).*

FIG. 3–28b *From GoGirl! by Trina Robbins and Anne Timmons. Copyright © 2002 by Trina Robbins and Anne Timmons. Reprinted by permission of the authors; Trina Robbins (<www.popimage.com/gogirl/>), Anne Timmons (<homepage.rnac.com/tafrin/>), Dark Horse Comics (<www.darkhorse.com/>).*

FIG. 3–29 *Spider-Man (Stan Lee and Steve Ditko),* Fantastic Firsts *(Marvel, 2002). Spider-Man and other Marvel Characters TM & © 2004 Marvel Characters, Inc. Used with permission.* <www.marvel.com/>.

FIG. 3–30 *Daredevil (Stan Lee and Bill Everett), Fantastic Firsts (Marvel, 2002). Daredevil and other Marvel characters TM & © 2004 Marvel Characters, Inc. Used with permission.* <www.marvel.com/>.

FIG. 3–31 *The Incredible Hulk (Stan Lee and Jack Kirby),* The Incredible Hulk: Beauty and the Behemoth *(Marvel, 1998). Hulk and other Marvel characters TM & © 2004 Marvel Characters, Inc. Used with permission. <www.marvel.com/>.*

anthology of stories from the 1960s. The Incredible Hulk: Beauty and the Behemoth (Marvel Comics, 1998) (Figure 3–31) offers readers a chance to chart the self-control issues of comics' very own Dr. Jekyll and Mr. Hyde, from his first appearance in 1962 through the late 1990s.

For a change of pace from the SLAM-BAM! of the action heroes, students can research five decades of teenage life in one of comics' favorite cities, Riverdale. The seven-volume Archie Americana Series (Archie Comic Publications, Inc.) offers reprints from the 1940s through the 1980s. Archie, Veronica, and Betty go from the jitterbug and sock hops to beatniks, surfing, miniskirts, sit-ins, and roller disco.

Expect some heated discussion and lots of passionate writing as students move beyond the Archie comics and compare and contrast the simple and generally danger-free life in Riverdale with the far more complicated and hazardous life of students living in Shanghai, Phnom Penh, Munich, Addis Ababa, Tehran, San Francisco, Atlanta, or Joplin, Missouri.

Comics from Scratch

Materials: comic-making supplies (paper, pencils, erasers . . .)

Description: Students work in small production teams and produce and publish original comic strips and comic books.

Topics and Strategies:
- teacher-made comics for modeling
- comics production steps
- material suggestions
- real comics for real readers

Background

Comics based activities offer several levels of student invention, from simple to elaborate and all stops in between. In Make-A-Title, students' creations may be only a word or two long. Take-A-Stand requires a full panel of artwork and a little writing. Scripting requires a complete story line. Students produce more writing in Fill-It-Up, and more dialogue and art in Missing Panels and Add-A-Panel.

This activity is the BIG project. Students create a comic from scratch and handle all aspects of production, including all the art and all the writing. How much time you and students devote to the project depends on the type of comics you'd like to produce.

Student-made comics generally fall into two categories: gag strips and content-based comic books. Strips are patterned after newspaper comics and feature contemporary settings, lots of humor, student-age characters, and the

FIG. 3–32 *Special Present. Sophie Lin, Perterson Middle School, Sunnyvale, California.*

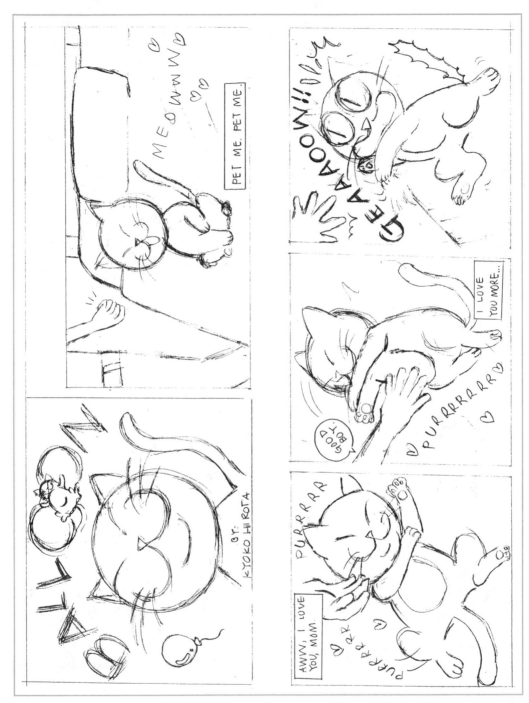

FIG. 3–33a *Balloon (strip) Kyoto Hirota , grade 11, Carlmont High School, Belmont, California.*

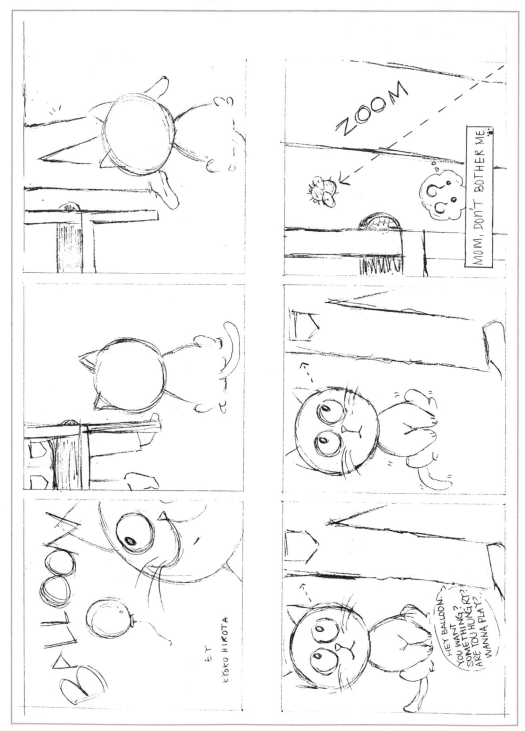

FIG. 3–33b *Balloon (strip) Kyoto Hirota , grade 11, Carlmont High School, Belmont, California.*

obligatory talking animals (see Figures 3–32, 3–33a & b). Comic books spring from current or recent units of study, for example, the Bill of Rights, the Great Depression, aerodynamics, weather systems, renewable energy sources, or an upcoming presidential election. See Chapter 4 for a variety of online student-made comics.

Though both varieties help with second language development, comic books also reinforce and extend subject-matter knowledge. Most teachers understandably favor content-based books over gag strips given the books' greater learning payoff. Doing a half dozen installments of a four-panel gag strip, however, requires far less time than producing an eight-page, fully researched, content-infused book. At an hour or so a day, comic strips can take a couple weeks to complete, comic books a couple months. Recommendation: If students can only spend ten to twenty hours on the project, go with strips. If forty or more hours are available, go with comic books.

Modeling and Teacher-Made Comics

Modeling each production step, though time-consuming, ensures higher-quality comics and increases the activity's language-learning mileage. Teachers new to comic making often feel they can't tackle the modeling—and the whole project—without the assistance of a professional comic artist. Certainly having a local artist visit the class and help is a plus; students pick up a number of useful hints and are always excited to work with the "genuine article." But help from a pro is not necessary.

Teachers don't have to draw like Elena Steier (Suzy Q, Toy Repair) or Stan Sakai (Usagi Yojimbo) (see Figure 3–34) and know the ins and outs of every production step to successfully guide students through the project. In fact, stick-figure drawings done by the teacher often inspire reluctant student artists more than those from a pro. Students know they can quickly match or surpass the drawing level of the teacher; drawing like the pro could take a lifetime.

Most teachers will find themselves learning the craft of comics making right alongside their students as they help design a splash page, make the dialogue punchier, hash out panel-to-panel transitions, and give some depth to flat drawings. Some teachers may want to create their own short comic. The benefits: You'll deepen your understanding of the process and produce modeling material for each production step. And you'll have fun! Don't be surprised if you suddenly double the length of the project once you figure out how to make a rabbit look like a rabbit instead of a cat with long ears, or make your Civil War soldiers look like they're fighting in the nineteenth rather than the twenty-first century. Students love to make comics; so do teachers once they take the plunge.

There's another significant but easily overlooked benefit in teacher-made comics. We talk to students a lot about what proficient learners do, how they go about learning what they need to learn, what strategies they use, and what they do when they hit a roadblock. Here's a chance for students to see a proficient learner in action—their teacher.

FIG. 3–34 *From* Usagi Yojimbo: Book 1 *by Stan Sakai. Copyright © 1987, 1999 by Stan Sakai. Reprinted by permission of Fantagraphics Books, Inc., <www.fantagraphics.com/>.*

Process

Comic-Book-Making Steps

This is the deluxe version of comic construction. If you've got the time, energy, and, most important, wide-scale student buy-in, you'll hit all or most of the ten steps in depth. Teachers wishing to devote less time to the activity or those testing the waters on student-made comics will skip a step or two or reduce the number of elements hit within steps. As with all activities in the book, this is a suggested route, not *the* route. Comic making can take myriad forms. The steps here provide a starting point only. Feel free to massage, expand, resequence, or delete elements as necessary.

Step One: Production Teams

Students (with some teacher guidance!) form production teams. Though pairs can get the job done, linguistically mixed groups of four to six students offer several advantages: First, there's more interaction, hence more opportunities to hear and use L2. Second, there's more L2 help available when second language learners hit a snag. Finally, groups replicate the real world of commercial production, where a number of people do specific jobs, pooling talents and skills to create and publish a comic. For the steps here, let's assume you've gone with small groups.

Step Two: Job Descriptions and Samples

The teacher briefly describes each team job and shows sample products. For example, "Here's what a penciller does and what his or her work looks like. Here's what the editor does and . . ." Samples are essential. Without the products—research pulled from the Web, pencil sketches, draft dialogue with editing marks, inked and colored drawings, finished caption lettering—job descriptions will make little to no sense for beginning and early intermediate students. Moreover, the samples help clarify project goal and process for all students, including native speakers. Samples show students where they're headed (to an original comic) and how they're going to get there (by completing various tasks),

In large commercial comics production, the general rule is one person to a job. The writer writes and the inker inks. In student-made comics, jobs are shared. One student may be the Lead Researcher or the Lead Editor, but all students are expected to learn the basics of each job, help get all the jobs done, and actively participate in each step of the production process. The jobs, in a nutshell:

Researcher: The researcher gathers background information for the story and checks facts.

Writer: The writer drafts and revises the script, all the comic's written text.

Penciller: The penciller is the chief artist and does the roughing in (first draft) and final versions of all pictures.

Inker: The inker traces over the pictures with black ink, adds shading when necessary, and erases any leftover pencil lines.

Colorist: The colorist adds color to the pencilled drawings.

Letterer: The letterer prints the words in captions and dialogue balloons.

Editor: The editor reviews all visual and written work for accuracy and consistency.

Step Three: T-Chart and Research

Once students understand the jobs and have chosen a topic for their comic, they make a T-chart. Let's imagine a group of eleventh graders working on the Great Depression. What students know about this period in American history goes on the left, questions about the period go on the right.

Great Depression	
FACTS	**QUESTIONS**
• stock market crash of 1929 •	• How many people lost money in the crash?
• by 1931, four to five million • unemployed	• How big a problem was hunger?
• familes in shantytowns •	• What was life like in shantytowns?
• Roosevelt—Works Progress • Administration (WPA)	• Did African Americans and Latinos get jobs with the WPA?

The questions spur additional research. As students find answers, they check off the questions and add new information to the what-we-know (FACTS) side of the T-chart.

As with any research-based activity, the students pull information from textbooks, trade books, the school library, classmates, local community experts, and the Internet. The nature of the information gathered, however, is slightly different with comics research: students often compile as much visual material as written. And for good reason. Comics are a visual medium; they live or die on their art. Accurate and detailed pictures advance a narrative; inaccurate and vague ones can kill it.

A group may know the key facts concerning Roosevelt's New Deal, depression-fighting strategies, but be clueless as to what the clothing, hairstyles, buildings, vehicles, tools, and furnishings of the era looked like. Without consulting good visual reference material, the first draft of their comic may show the president working out the details of the CCC (Civilian Conservation Corps) on a laptop. When the pictures ring false, so does the story.

Once the research is completed, students review their what-we-know list and circle the three facts they find most interesting. From those three they choose one fact to use as the centerpiece of their comic—for example, the fact that thousands of families lost their farms during the depression. Other interesting facts about the era may be woven into the comic, but only when those facts help elaborate the core story—one family losing a farm in the 1930s. Other groups in the room working on the depression might build stories around a businessman's suicide, a day in the life of a street vendor, the impact of a school closing on three high school friends, men setting a forest fire to generate work as firefighters, and Eleanor Roosevelt visiting coal miners in West Virginia. This single fact–single event approach helps students take a huge topic and whittle it down to size, to something that comfortably fits inside an eight-page comic, and most important, to something that's personally meaningful and memorable.

Step Four: Plotting

The writer begins with a log line, which summarizes the story in a single sentence, for example:

> The Hull family fights to keep their farm during the Great Depression in 1930s Iowa, but loses it in the end.

The log line is then expanded using a narrative template. A typical template includes:

- title (What the comic is about)
  - orientation
  - time
  - setting
  - characters (introduced)
- conflict/problem
- plan/action steps
- resolution/climax
- coda/moral

The template serves two essential functions: (1) it reminds writers of the key ingredients that go into a cohesive, strong, and satisfying story, and (2) it provides a basic plotting sequence for writer and penciller—what they'll write and draw toward the beginning, middle, and end of the comic.

Once the template items are filled in with a phrase or two each, the writer plots out the story per comic page. If the group wants to tell their story in eight pages, the distribution might be:

Page Plots	
Page 1:	the when, where, and who of the story (1930s, Iowa, the Hulls: Dad, Mom, and four kids)
Pages 2–3:	the conflict (farm prices fall 60 percent, bank foreclosure on Hull farm)
Pages 4–6:	action steps (trying to hang on to the family farm)
Page 7:	resolution/climax (family loses farm despite neighbors' help)
Page 8:	moral/coda/upshot (life doesn't always have a happy ending)

The writer then takes each plot page and parts out the story per individual panel, adding details along the way. By the end of the plotting step, with three to six panels a page, the writer has created twenty-five to fifty panel descriptions. For example, page 7 (resolution/climax) might read something like:

Panel Descriptions	
Panel 1:	Dad is riding a tractor, harvesting corn. He is hot, sweaty, and looks worn out. Robert and Paul (oldest kids) are at the edge of the cornfield trying to fix the truck. They can't get it to run.
Panel 2:	Mom is hanging laundry outside. She looks worn out like Dad. Andy (the youngest) tries to help mom but can't reach the clothesline. Rose (middle child) is inside the house, sweeping the kitchen.
Panel 3:	Mailman arrives with a letter from the bank.
Panel 4:	Mom walks to mailbox. Dad and kids watch her as she takes out the letter.
Panel 5:	Mom opens letter and starts to cry. Letter has FORECLOSURE printed on the top.

Step Five: Roughing In

The penciller takes the descriptions and goes to work, roughing in (lightly sketching) the main action of each panel, translating words into pictures. Background detail will come later. Pencillers and their assistants (other group members) will need some drawing support. Ironically—and sadly—the higher up you go in the grades, the more support is needed. In a class of thirty third graders, I may have a half dozen reluctant artists—the "I can't draw!" kids. By late high school, those numbers commonly flip. Out of thirty Juniors in an American History period, I may have only six artists. The other twenty-four students have convinced themselves they can't draw.

Teacher-made drawings, as suggested in the modeling section, will increase the number of student artists. When the teacher risks having her sketch of President Roosevelt mistaken for Eleanor, and Fala (the president's dog) mistaken for a buffalo, even the most unwilling artist in the room may pick up a pencil. Yet teachers and students new to cartooning may both need some pointers, especially if they'd like to move beyond flat, static, stick-figure cartooning. One place to get those pointers, beyond good how-to-draw books (see Chapter 4 for recommendations), is from a class artist-in-residence. The artist-in-residence might be an amateur; for example, a parent of one of your students who draws as a hobby, or a professional cartoonist. You can find a pro by checking with your local comics shop or art supply store. Ask for artist recommendations.

Most cartoonists jump at the chance to work with students and share what they know about their favorite art form. Amateur or pro, the artist-in-residence visits the class a couple times a week during the project and offers minilessons and guided practice on cartooning: warm-ups, shape starters, active stick figures, perspective, shading, and the basics of drawing people, animals, clothes, props, and backgrounds. One of the big problems in student drawings is rigidity. Motionless characters, looking more like sculptures than people, often fill panel after panel—for a whole comic. Drawing books and the artist-in-residence can offer several tips for creating movement.

Lacking books and a visiting cartoonist, here are two options for making characters look more alive than dead. One, have students pose for each another. If a panel description calls for a skier, one person in the group freezes into the "downhill skier" position. The penciller observes and pulls basic shapes and lines from the pose for the drawing. Two, have students use a small posable drawing manikin as a model for character action. The wooden manikins are inexpensive and available at most art supply stores.

Materials

Some suggestions on drawing materials: Basic number 2 pencils do the job. Mechanical pencils, however, hold their point and will eliminate the thousand trips to the pencil sharpener. Make sure students use pencils with medium soft lead (HB or B). This grade produces a strong line and easily erases. Easy erasing is especially important if drawings are to be inked. Students will be doing lots of erasing and standard pencil erasers will be shot in no time flat. Have plenty of separate erasers on hand—art gum or the kneaded variety.

Any sort of unlined white paper will do, including newsprint. The size of the paper, however, is a different matter. With four to six panels on a page, standard letter-size paper is generally too small to work with, especially for lower-grade students. Drawings are abbreviated and the lettering is often so tiny or cramped that it's illegible. Legal-size paper offers a bit more room, but not enough to make a significant difference. When possible, use larger-format paper (eleven-by-seventeen-inch). Large panels can be photoreduced to fit the dimensions of a smaller end-product comic.

If you only have small paper to work with, take heart. Simply have students do one or at most two panels per 8.5-by-11-inch sheet. This option avoids squashed art and lettering and allows more than one student in the group to work on the drawings at a time. It also minimizes the number of drawings lost in an erasing disaster, where the penciller, letterer, or colorist rips a hole in a page of six drawings big enough to drive a school bus through. There may still be disasters, but when they strike, only a couple drawings will be ruined. Once all panels done on the smaller-size paper are finished, they are clipped, photoreduced, and pasted (use a noncurling glue like rubber cement) onto 8.5-by-11-inch backing sheets. One last paper option to consider: Skip paper altogether and use three-by-five or four-by-six-inch index cards.

An important reminder to all pencillers when roughing in: Leave room for captions and dialogue!

Step Six: Captions and Dialogue

Working from the written panel descriptions and the penciller's roughs, the writer creates a first draft of captions and dialogue. Captions, typically placed inside rectangles (or runners) at the top of a panel, provide information on character background, setting, and time shifts. Dialogue, placed in different types of word balloons, tell what characters say, think, and feel.

This first draft of the text is done on the same sheet as the panel descriptions (below or to the right of each description), *not* on the panel roughs. Words and visuals will change during the revision process, and adding words to the drawings at this point will increase project time and frustrate students. As words change, the penciller will have to erase and redraw, and as drawings change, the letterer will have to erase and reletter.

Step Seven: Editing and Revision

The editor checks the first draft of pictures and text for accuracy and consistency. Basic visual checks include making sure a character with long hair and a beard in one panel isn't suddenly bald and smooth-faced in the next. Content checks are tougher since they require subject matter knowledge. When group drafts show Cortés conquering Cuba, Rosa Parks holding on to her airplane seat, or the CIA supporting democratically elected Salvador Allende, editors catch the errors. At least we hope they do! If not, the teacher as editor-in-chief intervenes, and groups revise their pictures and text accordingly.

In addition to checking visuals and content facts, the editor reads captions and dialogue for meaning. The guiding question: Does this make sense? Garbled text is returned to the writer for a fix-up. Teacher objectives related to specific student language needs also guide the editor's work. A teacher might ask editors to zero in on two or three items in the first draft; for example, subject-verb agreement, possessives, and the use of key content vocabulary. Second drafts might be checked for pronoun reference and irregular past tense verbs.

Throughout the revision process, writer and penciller carefully coordinate efforts. The writer's words must clarify and augment the pictures. Too little text may leave the reader wondering what happened where and when, and to what character. Two much text may overwhelm second language beginners and make picture content irrelevant for advanced learners. The penciller's visuals must strike a similar balance. Too little detail in the pictures may leave L2 beginners struggling to understand the basic story line. Too much detail may decrease their motivation to dig into the captions and dialogue and do more reading in the second language. Words and pictures must work together to tell a clear and compelling story. The key—and challenge—is matching the right words with the right pictures. When that match is made, the whole becomes greater than the sum of its parts, and the unique communicative power of the comic art form is evident to students and teacher alike.

Based on feedback from the editor, group members, and teacher, the penciller and writer revise their drawings and text, have them checked one last time, attend to any final fix-ups, and give their finished work to the letterer.

Step Eight: Lettering, Inking, and Coloring

Like the pencillers, letterers can use sharp number 2 pencils. For consistently crisp and readable text, however, nothing beats a good mechanical pencil. Move to a thicker pencil (.7 mm) if heavy-handed letterers keep breaking the more standard .5 mm lead.

An alternative to lettering is to do all the text on computer, print it out, then snip and paste everything into the caption blocks and word balloons. Though the computer saves some time, the results are disappointing. One of the elements that makes a comic a comic instead of a brochure, catalogue, magazine, newspaper, book, or phone bill is the hand lettering. Computer-generated text won't give student creations the hand-crafted look of professional comics. I ask students to use the computer to draft and polish their text, if they wish, but to hand letter their captions and dialogue.

In commercial comics, the lettering is nearly always all caps. If one of your language targets is capitalization, have students use upper- and lowercase letters. An alternative that retains the look of professional comics is to use all caps, but have the letterer trace over bona fide caps in red pencil.

After the comic is fully drawn, written, and lettered, it's ready for inking. Fine-tipped felt markers like Pilot Razor Point pens will do the job. Whether the job needs to be done, however, is the important question. Inking is essential for producing sharp images in commercial comics. But unless students are after a highly polished product, think twice before having groups put pen to paper, especially newsprint. I've seen many drawings smudged, smeared, and completely ruined by inking. Ink disasters cut across the grades; some tenth graders can destroy an entire panel as fast as second graders. If a group is determined to ink, suggest they play it safe and ink copies of their drawings, not the originals. If disaster hits, reinking another copy will be less time-consuming than redoing a drawing. You'll also have fewer inkers and pencillers in tears. Even without the smudges and smears, inking sometimes degrades small drawings and detailed artwork. My recommendation: Skip inking whenever possible.

Finally, the comic goes to the colorist. Colored pencils work best. Their fine points permit the filling of small areas, and they erase—a huge plus. Crayons are workable for larger nondetailed drawings. But once that cow is colored blue, she stays blue. Felt-tipped markers are the least favored coloring tools in non-commercial settings. They provide brilliant color, but as with any type of inking, can have ruinous, detail-killing results. With markers, not only does the cow stay blue, she may become a nondescript blob of blue.

When I'm in a classroom and see lots of markers sitting in tubs on the tables, I'll often suggest that students forgo coloring their comics. I tell kids that coloring is time-consuming and that they run the risk of really messing up their drawings with markers. I describe the drama and power in simple pencil drawings and tell them how much I love black and white comics (which is true). All this to little avail, of course. A good half the class will have the caps off their markers before I finish extolling the virtues of non-colored comics. If groups are set on markers and you can't talk them into colored pencils, have the colorists, just like the inkers, color copies of the drawings, not the originals.

Step Nine: Finishing

At this point, student comics are nearly ready for publication. Only four finishing tasks remain: covers, splash page, page numbers, and binding. Front and back covers are frequently in color even when the artwork inside is all black and white. If students were dying to use markers, but put them aside at your urging, here's where they can use them. The front cover features the title and a large picture, often action-filled and with little to no text. Cover art should grab and pull the reader inside.

Students can save time on the cover art by copying and enlarging a scene from one of the panels. For the back, some groups go with a blank cover or only a small publication logo. Others, however, taking their cue from commercial comics, design a full-fledged ad for the back cover, complete with product hype, fake star endorsements, and a toll-free number to Order Your Rocket Shoes Now!

The splash page is page one, panel one of the comic. Like the cover, it features a large, high-interest visual, sets the scene, introduces one or more characters, and makes the reader want to turn the page to find out more (see Figure 3–35). Near the bottom of the splash page, students letter in production job credits, for example:

Michelle Chang (researcher)
Amelia Tejeda (editor)
Bobby Hall (writer)
Enrique Rivera (penciller)
Brian Obana (letterer)
Suzie Gustafson (inker and colorist)

Some groups skip a splash page and begin their comic with the original page one and its standard-size drawings. In this case, production credits are placed on the inside of the front or back cover. Please note: If students add a splash page, they'll need to renumber pages.

Though student-made comics have few pages by commercial standards, those six to eight pages can be jumbled in the hustle and bustle of production. Even easier to jumble are thirty to fifty panels when drawn on separate sheets of paper (or index cards) by different group members. Recommendation: Have students take a pencil and lightly number all pages and all panels, even when they assure you they're the most capable comic makers on planet Earth and that no numbers are needed. Numbers are needed.

FIG. 3–35 *Balloon (splash page). Kyoko Hirota, grade 11, Carlmont High School, Belmont, California.*

Finally, groups bind their comics, either as stand-alone stories or as a group of stories in a class anthology. Stand-alone stories have a real advantage during free voluntary reading; several students can read them at a time. Teachers, however, may prefer an anthology when students are willing to donate their comics to the class and when all the stories relate to the same curriculum topic or unit.

Individual titles are easily bound with staples or glue. Use colored tape at the edge to provide additional strength and to cover up the staples and glue streaks. Anthologies may be forty or fifty pages long and usually require a three-ring binder. Consider using plastic sheet protectors; they eliminate the hole punching and preserve the comics for years to come.

Once bound, be prepared for the inevitable "Whose comic is it?" question. If the comic is well done, everybody in the group will want it. One comic for five or six students almost guarantees a conflict. An easy, if imperfect, solution is to run off as many copies as you need, then draw names out of a hat for the original.

One last note: If the comic will be published on a student, class, or school website, scan before binding.

Step Ten: Publishing and Distribution

Student comics are considered published when they receive the official class imprint, for example:

> Volume One, Number One, March 18, 2004
> Published by The Fearless Frogs Group
> Ms. Isabel Garza's Third Period American History Class
> Ellington High School
> 451 Harris Ave.
> San Jose, California 95124

The imprint, issued by the teacher after final checking, is hand lettered or typed on a small piece of paper and glued to the inside cover.

Distribution helps student comics find an audience. Readers turn what could be mere academic exercise into an authentic literacy project. The comics first make the rounds group to group in the classroom. From there, they travel to other classes and perhaps into the school library for a month-long stay. Distribution beyond the school is time-consuming and logistically a lot trickier. So why bother?

Throughout the project, students have worked like real comics creators, essentially following the same process and doing the same jobs as in a commercial production. That real-world, get-the-project-done-like-the-pros orientation increases student interest and motivation, boosts L2 usage, and improves second language skills.

Real comics have real readers. Teacher and classmates, of course, count as real readers. But as one young budding comics artist reminded me recently, "They're not *as* real" as readers outside the school. What I believe underpins that sentiment is the fact that in most classrooms, students aren't able to choose what they read. With a few exceptions—a short daily period of free-choice reading in the elementary grades or a middle or high school literature list with a few optional titles—students read what teachers want them to read, or perhaps better said, what a district or state curriculum committee wants them to read. This young man knew that when people, even the teacher, read for pleasure outside school, they choose their own material. In school, a teacher's got to read student-produced work whether she wants to or not; it's her job. But away from school, if a teacher, or, for that matter, a mechanic, attorney, gardner, trucker, computer chip manufacturer—anybody—chooses to read the boy's comic, then he's snagged the genuine article: a real reader. To find those outside readers, the comics can become part of a family literacy project, exhibited at back-to-school night or circulated among parents and the local community using a library-type checkout system.

For increased readership, scanned comics move into cyberspace. Computer savvy students create their own websites and offer the comics as featured content. Other students might use an existing class or school website as their electronic display rack. Lots of students like to send their creations to family and friends as email attachments. Internet readers might live next door, across the country, or across the world. One important guideline for students: Know the person you're emailing. Student comics are great fun to read, but not as spam.

Quick Takes

Here are some additional activities for using comics in the multilingual classroom. All are spin-offs of activities already discussed in depth.

Free Voluntary Reading (FVR)
Students are offered comics as part of the mix of materials during daily free reading time. In addition to increasing the motivation to read, FVR improves reading comprehension, writing, grammar, vocabulary, and spelling (Elley 1991; Krashen 1993, 2003). Three keys to ensuring those literacy gains and making comics work in FVR: (1) provide a wide range of genres and text levels; (2) make sure students see you occasionally reading a comic to give this type of material the teacher seal-of-approval; and (3) keep FVR truly free and voluntary.

In many schools, FVR is referred to as SSR (Sustained Silent Reading). I was recently in a school that had dramatically altered the first S. SSR was now *Supervised* Silent Reading and it was teachers—not students—who made most of the decisions about what was read.

Between the Panels
Students work alone or in pairs reading comics in two ways: (1) reading only in-panel pictures and text, and (2) reading in-panel *and* off-panel pictures and text. In comics, action and dialogue take place inside the panels and also between panels. Off-panel happenings are filled in by the reader's imagination based on in-panel action and dialogue. Reading the space between panels (or the "gutter" in comics parlance) is critical to comprehending the comic.

Standard written text works much the same way. Proficient readers continually infer, "reading between the lines" by using all the available text clues and cues to fill in their knowledge gaps. With this activity, students soon realize that their comprehension—and enjoyment!—of comics greatly improve the more they infer, the more on- and off-panel reading they do. See Figure 3–36 for a comic I recently used with some middle schoolers at the early intermediate level. Once we added off-panel reading to reading the pictures and text, several students reported an increase in understanding.

Power Words

Students periodically mine favorite comic strips for "power words." Power words are freely chosen and, hence, personally meaningful. These are words students want to remember—and use—to make their speech and writing more communicative. Power words can be categorized into word families and placed in word banks. Some students like to snip a strip out of the paper (or print it off the Web), highlight the target word, and paste the strip into a notebook. Pasted strips provide a meaning-making context for each word, especially important when students are dealing with dozens of new words and need a reminder on how a word pulled from a comic three or four months ago is used. Lower-grade teachers sometimes have students incorporate personal power words into class spelling and word study activities.

Storyboarding

Students fill a set of panels with pictures and text. This strategy is particularly helpful when the sequencing of events is critical, for example, in retelling a story, describing a science experiment, or sorting out historical eras and developments (see Figures 3–37, 3–38a, and 3–38b).

Noodling

Students take notes during teacher's direct instruction with a combination of text and small drawings. Notes + doodles = noodling. The techique is sometimes called a "chalk-talk" and is applicable to any content area. The drawings put a concrete face on abstract oral and written language. Getting students to adopt the technique depends in large part on the teacher's willingness to draw in front of students. Never fear: You don't need to be a professional artist to noodle. Simply go with stick figures. They work!

What Would Snoopy Say?

Students assume the identity of a favorite comic strip or comic book character and role-play a short response to an event (often a dilemma) outside the world of comics. The response can be oral or written. The events may come from a class literature book, history text, or current newspaper or TV report. I asked

---

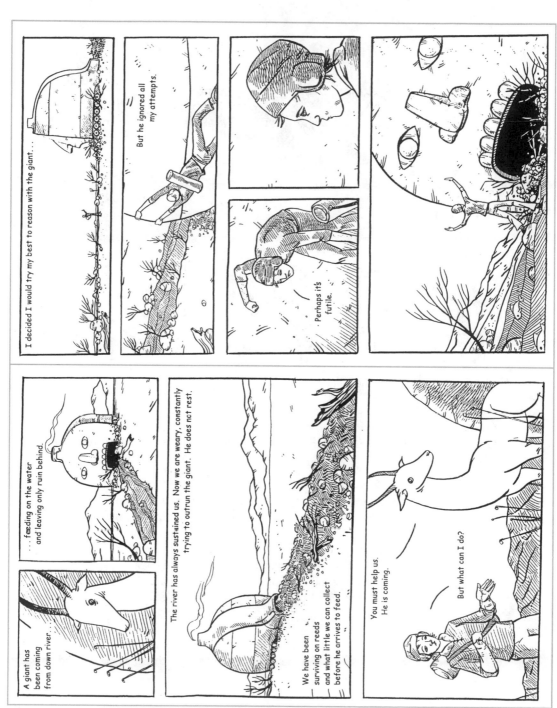

FIG. 3–36 "Trail of Waste" by Andy Gouveia originally published in Garish Zow Comics (no.2). Copyright © 2002 by Andy Gouveia. Reprinted with permission of Hidden Agenda Press, <www.hiddenagendapress.com/>.

FIG. 3–37 *History of Money. Abraham Ramos, grade 3, Hawthorne Elementary School, Oakland, California.*

some fourth- and fifth-grade students who had been reading comic strips for several weeks what particular characters would do about the terrible traffic problem in the San Francisco Bay Area. Some responses (edited):

LUANN: Share rides with boyfriend.
JEREMY (from Zits): No problem because cars are cool!
MOM (in Dennis the Menace): Put cars in the corner for being bad.
SNOOPY: Get away from traffic. Move to the desert!

Act-It-Out

Students work in pairs or small groups and act out favorite comic strips. Making the mini-plays comprehensible for students with beginning second language proficiency requires heavy contextualizing—props, costumes, visuals, sound effects, and movement. Groups need time to make and scrounge required items. With high-interest, comprehensible strips, students need little encouragement to expand on the given text. Many let go of the memorized dialogue altogether and improvise their way through the play. Students without acting parts can be "narrators" and read the strips' captions. No captions? Have students create them.

Autobiography

Using a comic strip or comic book format, students retell key events in their lives. Depending on interest level and available time for the activity, students may retell a single memorable event or create full autobiographies. Middle and high school students may want to take a look at Katherine Arnoldi's *The Amazing True Story of a Teenage Single Mom* (Figures 3–39a, 3–39b, 3–39c) to get a sense of the expressive power in autobiographical comics.

Character Interviews

Students in small groups choose a character from a favorite strip, comic book, or graphic novel, research the character, then collectively play the part of that character as they respond to interview questions. Questions can be posed by the teacher or other groups of students.

Character Report Card

Students develop behavior-based report cards for favorite comics characters. Figure 3–40 shows a card for Garfield, created by Omri, a third-grade student in one of Beth Hawley's ESL classes at Cairo American College in Cairo, Egypt. Omri chose the categories, designed a grading scale, assigned ratings, and added a comment section to explain three of the lowest ratings. He even included a small health update. I think Garfield's owner, Jon, would agree with Omri's assessment. Clearly, Garfield could stand an attitude adjustment. And fewer cakes and cookies.

Pet-to-Pet

Students compare and contrast their pets with animal counterparts in the comics, looking at physical characteristics, disposition, habits, likes and dislikes. Dogs and cats abound in the comics. But what about students with other, less common pets? Not a problem. Here's a sampling of other creatures and where they live in the comics.

> bird (in Ziggy)
> duck (Bob the Duck in Drabble)
> ferret (Fungo in Get Fuzzy)
> fish (Ernest in Sherman's Lagoon)

Field Sketch: Storyboarding

Darlene Rodriguez's fourth graders use storyboards as a preliminary to acting out and videoing Native American legends.

Students hear the legends, visualize the pictures in their minds, and then talk about the legends in pairs or small groups. Then the storyboards are created. The challenge is always the vocabulary, but this method and strategy is usually successful with children who are beginning to grasp the English language. They enjoy this creative step leading to formulating simple stories, fables, and legends. I've taught for thirty-six years and keep this strategy alive year after year because of the results I get in language acquisition.

—Darlene Rodriguez, Teacher
Thousand Oaks School
Berkeley, California

Field Sketch: Noodling the Classics

One strategy I use I call noodling, a cross between notetaking and doodling. I learned the strategy from a Sheltered English teacher. Before we begin reading *Romeo and Juliet*, I tell the students the story, illustrating it on the board at the same time. I use symbols and stick figures, and a few words here and there. Students copy the drawings into their notebooks, and then write a summary of the story as homework. It's very gratifying to see how detailed their summaries are, and they feel good about themselves because they "understand" Shakespeare after only one day. I've also used the strategy for *Hamlet* and *The Odyssey*.

—Marna Bynum, English Teacher
Merrill F. West High School
Tracy, California

FIG. 3–38a *Miwok Legend (Tis-Sé-Yak). Alaytra Johnson, Terry Carter, and Samson Higano, grade 4, Thousand Oaks School, Berkeley, California.*

The man and woman froze from wickedness

Then turned into stone.

Northdome and Half dome is what they are today

FIG. 3–38b *Miwok Legend (Tis-Sé-Yak). Alaytra Johnson, Terry Carter, and Sumson Higuno, grade 4, Thousand Oaks School, Berkeley, California.*

FIG. 3–39a *From* The Amazing True Story of a Teenage Single Mom *by Katherine Arnoldi. Copyright © 1998 by Katherine Arnoldi. Reprinted by permission of Hyperion.*

FIG. 3–39b *From* The Amazing True Story of a Teenage Single Mom *by Katherine Arnoldi. Copyright © 1998 by Katherine Arnoldi. Reprinted by permission of Hyperion.*

FIG. 3–39c *From* The Amazing True Story of a Teenage Single Mom *by Katherine Arnoldi. Copyright © 1998 by Katherine Arnoldi. Reprinted by permission of Hyperion.*

REPORT CARD

Student Name: Garfield   Evaluation by: Omri

Kindness	3	Follows directions	2	Works independently	1
Effort	1	Cooperation	1	Positive attitude	1
Manners	1	Makes good use of time	5	Health	2

GRADING SCALE

1 Unacceptable
2 Unsatisfactory
3 Satisfactory
4 Good
5 Excellent

COMMENTS [unedited]: I gave Garfield low grade on effort because he's sleepy and doesn't pay attention. I gave Garfield low grade on manners because he always hits Odie. I gave Garfield low grade on following directions because he doesn't follows Jon's directions.

HEALTH

Ears: Garfield's ears are small but his hearing is O.K.
Eyes: Garfield needs glasses
Height: Garfield's height is 7 centimeters
Weight: Garfield eats a lot and fat because of this his weight is 56 KG.
Teeth: Normal.

Omri, third grade. Beth Hawley, ESL Teacher. Grades 1–5. Cairo American College. Cairo, Egypt.

FIG. 3–40 *Garfield Report Card*

gecko (Moki in Gecko Tales)
hermit crab (Hawthorne in Sherman's Lagoon)
horse (Lucy in Non Sequitur)
iguana (Quincy in FoxTrot)
pig (in Pearls Before Swine)
rabbit (Matt's Rabbit)
rat (Morty & Max)
snake (Snake Tales)
spider (in Garfield)
turtle (Aford)

Write the Artist

Students write letters or email to their favorite comics artists. Most artists will write back. Thought-provoking questions about characters or a particular turn or twist in a story arc will increase the chances (and size) of a response. The classic "How did you learn to draw like that?!" gets old fast.

Resources

teaching is a lot like house painting: preparation is half the work. Before the first coat is applied, painters spend hours scraping, sanding, and taping. Before the next unit or instructional approach is implemented, teachers spend hours (and a fair number of their weekends!) planning, researching, and scrounging materials. Locating the resources and materials you'll need for comics-based activities can be especially time-consuming. And frustrating. Traditional material sources—public library, chain bookstore, teacher supply store, and the packrat colleague down the hall—won't have all the comics you need. Or worse, won't have anything you need.

After staff development workshops where I feature comics, I often hear from teachers searching for materials. They're excited about using comics with their second language learners but can't find those "just-right" titles—right genre, topic, age and reading level. One teacher recently wanted comic books on the Civil War for his L2 middle schoolers, another wanted wordless graphic novels for her adult ed ESL students. A third needed reduced-text sci-fi and fantasy titles for several of his fourth-grade reluctant readers. After a long, generally unsuccessful hunt, all these teachers were ready to give up on comics before they'd begun.

This chapter offers a smorgasbord of resources arranged in five major categories: Comics Reviews, Online Reviews, Online Comics, Comics in Other Languages, and the miscellaneous catch-all, Other. Each major category is divided into several subcategories. This arrangement with the accompanying resource annotations will help you quickly locate what you need. Quicker access to materials will, in turn, dramatically reduce your preparation time for comics-based activities.

Comics Reviews

Teachers new to comics typically ask about the variety of available materials. This section tries to answer the "What's out there?" question. "Tries" is the key word. Given the thousands of cartoons, comic strips, comic books, and graphic novels published each year, any review list is cursory at best. What follows offers a taste of what's available in the vast world of comics, but is a starting point only. Please see the resources listed at the end of this section for many more reviews. The materials reviewed here, mostly graphic novels, are comics I've used in various settings or have seen used by other teachers and feel comfortable recommending. My apologies to anyone whose favorite comic didn't make the list. I know I'll hear grumbles from the Archie and Zippy partisans within a week of publication!

Each review provides a short content summary and grade and language proficiency indicators. Most include hints on using the material with second language learners. A caveat on the grade and language proficiency indicators: Like most experienced teachers, I have a good idea as to what books work with first graders versus fifth or tenth graders. And like most teachers who have taught a lot of second language learners, I have a good idea of what books fly with beginning versus intermediate or advanced L2 readers. A good idea perhaps, but far from perfect. Students still fool me, some benefiting from material whose content and reading level I'd pegged as too adult and too difficult, others benefiting from material I'd pegged as too juvenile and too easy. I recall the third grader who sat for fifteen minutes, slowly paging through a Smithsonian magazine, absolutely mesmerized, reading what he could and guiltlessly skipping what he couldn't. I also remember the adult intermediate ESL student who couldn't get enough Looney Tune comics.

Though experienced teachers guess right on materials more than they guess wrong, we can't always know what content, writing format, or drawing style will capture the interest of all our students. The grade and language proficiency indicators in the reviews are therefore rough estimates, best guesses on my part. I've used a five-level scale for language proficiency: beginning, early intermediate, intermediate, early advanced, and advanced, running from square-one, nonreaders in English to students reading at a near-native level. Reviews are alphabetical, by title.

Age of Reptiles: Tribal Warfare by Ricardo Delgado. 1996. Milwaukie, OR: Dark Horse Comics.

Material: graphic novel (wordless)
Genre: animal action adventure
Age level: grade 3 and above
Language level: all

It's an eat-or-be-eaten dinosaur world, and when a deinonychus group steals a T-Rex's eggs, it's dinner time! Action-packed from start to finish, this suspenseful romp through Cretaceous America will leave you breathless and wanting more of Delgado's splendid color drawings and another great dino story. Fortunately, you get both in the follow-up *Age of Reptiles: The Hunt* (1997).

I shared these titles with a third-grade teacher last year who expressed some concern about the violence. Animals are attacked, bleed, and die in Delgado's books. So goes nature. His third graders loved them.

Akira (Vol. 1) by Katsuhiro Otomo. 2000. Milwaukie, OR: Dark Horse Comics.

Material: graphic novel
Genre: sci-fi adventure
Age level: high school to adult
Language level: early intermediate

If your high school students find Archie comics too tame and the superhero titles too tough a read, have them give Akira a whirl.

Teenage protagonists, fast motorcycles, and action-heavy adventures in a dangerous post-apocalyptic Tokyo will grab the most jaded—or print-overwhelmed—second language learner. Once grabbed, there's plenty more Akira. Otomo's sci-fi epic stretches to six volumes and over 2,000 pages. The books are pricey at around twenty-five dollars a volume, but used copies are plentiful on the Web.

The Amazing True Story of a Teenage Single Mom by Katherine Arnoldi. 1998. New York: Hyperion. (See Figures 3–39a–c on pages 152–54.)

Material: graphic novel
Genre: memoir
Age level: middle school to adult
Language level: intermediate

We've all experienced some hardships in our lives. Artist Katherine Arnoldi, however, has had more than her fair share. This riveting memoir recounts Arnoldi's struggles in overcoming childhood neglect, poverty, sexual violence, dead-end jobs, illness, and despair. Here's life in the raw, messy, real, and without a speck of sugar coating. Weaker souls may have simply called it quits; Arnoldi perseveres, ultimately managing what once seemed impossible: leaving the ugly past behind, becoming a great mom, and realizing her dream of going to college. Her tale of personal triumph will interest—and instruct—any student feeling beaten and trapped by adversity. Arnoldi points the way up and out.

Baldo: The Lower You Ride, The Cooler You Are by Hector Cantú and Carlos Castellanos. 2001. Kansas City, MO: Andrews McMeel.

Material: comic strips
Genre: humor
Age level: middle school to adult
Language level: early intermediate to advanced

Join the Bermudez family for nonstop fun and frolic. There's Baldo, always on the quest for a low rider and that still more elusive teen necessity, coolness; little sister Gracie and her shouts of Chica Power!; and Tía Carmen with her ghosts, psychic hotline, chickens in the kitchen, and telenovela (soap opera) addiction. Finally, there's steadfast, long-suffering dad trying his best to keep the lid on the works while wondering if Baldo's T-shirt emblazoned with "Low Rider" refers to his son's car interest or his pants.

The strips dealing with the frustrations—and dangers—of relying on children as translators will be especially funny and meaningful to your second language students. (See Figure 3–9 on page 92.)

Barefoot Gen: A Cartoon Story of Hiroshima by Keiji Nakazawa. 2003. San Francisco: Last Gasp.

Material: graphic novel
Genre: historical fiction
Age level: middle school to adult
Language level: early intermediate to early advanced

Barefoot Gen tells the story of the American bombing of Hiroshima from a Japanese perspective. Gen is a young boy with a dad who is staunchly antimilitarist. When the dad is arrested for pacifist statements, Gen and the entire Nakaoka family are branded traitors. The family, already dealing with a serious wartime lack of basic necessities including food, must now endure rejection, taunting, and bullying by pro-war friends and neighbors. The real terror hits on August 6, 1945, when the atomic bomb nicknamed "Little Boy" explodes over Hiroshima. Buildings evaporate, homes collapse, flesh melts, and an inferno rages through the city (see Figure 4–1). Three images stayed with me long after I finished the book: a horse on fire, a little girl blinded by flying glass, and Gen's dad, brother, and sister trapped and dying in the rubble.

Barefoot Gen is a powerful antiwar, antinuclear weapons statement. It's also an autobiographical tale; author Nakazawa was seven when his hometown was incinerated. Three more volumes complete the Gen saga: *The Day After* (Vol. 2); *Life After the Bomb* (Vol. 3); and *Out of the Ashes* (Vol. 4).

FIG. 4–1 *From* Barefoot Gen: A Cartoon Story of Hiroshima *by Keiji Nakazawa. Copyright ©
1987 by Keiji Nakazawa. Reprinted with permission from Last Gasp of San Francisco, 777
Florida St., San Francisco, CA, 94110, <www.lastgasp.com/>.*

The Big Book of Urban Legends by various authors/artists. 1994.
New York: Paradox Press.

Material: short stories (anthology)
Genre: legends (urban)
Age level: high school to adult
Language level: beginning to early advanced

These two hundred urban legends, most told in a single page of eight or nine panels, range from the supernatural ("The Vanishing Hitchhiker"; see Figure 4–2), the creepy ("The Spider in the Hairdo"), and the gross ("The Mouse in the Coke Bottle") to the frightening ("The Hook"), the absurd ("Alligators in the Sewer"), and the mysterious ("The Unstealable Car"). Several tame sex-based legends are included in the mix.

If you're looking for material for older students to spur L2 conversation and writing, these classic, too-good-to-be-true stories will do the trick. After reading and discussing a few legends, students will want to share alternative versions of the same stories as well as additional tales from their home countries.

The book features the work of 196 different artists, which makes it a must read (and a must have!) for any student or teacher who's a comic art fan.

Blood Song by Eric Drooker. 2002. San Diego, CA: Harcourt.

Material: graphic novel (wordless)
Genre: adventure/urban drama
Age level: high school to adult
Language level: all

Without warning, soldiers descend on an idyllic Southeast Asian village and burn it to the ground. One young woman and her faithful dog survive and flee into the forest. They make their way to the coast, find a boat, and escape to sea. A whirlpool carries them to the other side of the world where survival in the big city is nearly as difficult and dicey as in the home country.

Blood Song is wordless. But not for long. The story, with its themes of oppression, resistance, and renewal, told in dramatic black and light

FIG. 4–2 *"The Vanishing Hitchhiker" from* The Big Book of Urban Legends *by Nghia Lam. Copyright © 1994 Paradox Press, an imprint of DC Comics. Reprinted by permission of DC Comics, <www.dccomics.com/>. All rights reserved.*

blue panels with the occasional splash of brillant color, will have students talking and writing from the first page. At one point in the tale a street musician stands on a small wooden box playing for a large, appreciative crowd. He wails soulfully and a hot, yellow-orange light streams out of his tenor sax. The young woman and dog dance to the joyous music. Suddenly the police arrive and disperse the crowd, then knock the musician to the sidewalk and confiscate his instrument. Try reading those pictures with a partner and *not* talking.

Bone Volume One: Out from Boneville by Jeff Smith. 1996. Columbus, OH: Cartoon Books.

Material: graphic novel
Genre: fantasy adventure
Age level: middle school and up
Language level: early intermediate

The Bone cousins—Fone, Phoney, and Smiley—offer an ideal comedic mix of the trustworthy, the crooked, and the just plain silly. The oddball trio is thrown out of Boneville, lose their way in the desert, and stumble on a valley as strange and forbidding as it is beautiful. That's when the real fun and mystery begin.

You can use Bone to target an important, though often neglected, area in ESL: colloquialisms. The dialogue reflects how native speakers use English during informal conversation, packed with contractions (that's, should've, how'd), compressions (wanna, whaddya, outta), and reduced forms ('cause, 'em, ya). Bone books (nine in the series and counting) offer students a convenient vehicle for comparing and contrasting "book English" with "street English."

Broad Appeal: An Anthology of Comics for Everyone by various women artists. 2003. Pasadena, CA: Friends of Lulu.

Material: short stories (anthology)
Genres: various
Age level: middle school to adult
Language level: beginning to advanced

Myths about comics are as hard to kill as garden weeds. At each teacher workshop I do on comics, I pull as many myths up by the roots as I can. By the next workshop, they've invariably grown back. One of the most tenacious myths is that girls and women don't read or produce comics, commonly phrased as, "It's a guy thing." This anthology, featuring nearly four dozen female artists, should help with weed control. The selections cover a wide range of genres, from wordless, fantasy, and teen to adventure, political, and contemporary narrative (see Figure 4–3a & b).

If you've got students wanting and needing an alternative perspective to the world of Betty and Veronica (Archie comics), try Janet Hetherington's I Was a Teen-Aged Love Zombie! or Shaenon Garrity's Alien Watching.

FIG. 4–3a *"50 Years of War in Drawn Books" from* Broad Appeal: An Anthology of Comics for Everyone, Friends of Lulu *by Donna Barr. Copyright © 2002 by Donna Barr. Reprinted by permission of the author,* (<www.stinz.com/home/>), *Friends of Lulu* (<www.friends-lulu.org/>).

FIG. 4–3b *"50 Years of War in Drawn Books" from* Broad Appeal: An Anthology of Comics for Everyone, Friends of Lulu *by Donna Barr. Copyright © 2002 by Donna Barr. Reprinted by permission of the author, (<www.stinz.com/home/>), Friends of Lulu (<www.friends-lulu.org/>).*

Cave-In by Brian Ralph. 1999. Cambridge, MA: Highwater Books.

Material: graphic novel (wordless)
Genre: fantasy adventure
Age level: grade 2 and above
Language level: all

A resourceful young boy journeys through a strange, often hazardous underground world and is befriended by an Egyptian mummy along the way. The cave-in sequence is a thrill-ride—and a heartbreaker. Tender, light-hearted moments help balance the sad. The drawings are detailed but not overly busy (Figure 4–4).

FIG. 4–4 *From* Cave-In *by Brian Ralph. Copyright © 1999 by Brian Ralph. Reprinted by permission of Highwater Books,* <www.highwaterbooks.com/index.html>.

Combustion by Chris Lanier. 1999. Seattle, WA: Fantagraphics Books.

> **Material:** graphic novel (wordless)
> **Genre:** war
> **Age level:** middle school and above
> **Language level:** all

A militarist state colonizes a small island nation. When the island citizens rebel, paratroopers are dropped in to suppress the uprising. A freak wind carries one trooper far away from his comrades. He lands in a forest, reconnoiters, rests, and is suddenly attacked. The trooper kills the rebel attacker, another lone soldier who has lost his way, then sits beside the bloody body reflecting on war and death. The hours pass. Melancholy turns to remorse and ultimately to compassion for the enemy. The soldier lays his rifle on the ground and walks out of the forest and up a hill. At the crest he looks down upon a bombed and burning village. Lanier's black and white woodcuts shape a cautionary tale about the dangers—and horrors—of unbridled nationalism.

A few of your second language learners may want to share their personal or family war stories after reading the comic. Be prepared for some "combustible" material, whether oral or written. Some of the student anecdotes will equal Lanier's tale horror for horror; some will surpass it.

Dead End by Thomas Ott. 2002. Seattle, WA: Fantagraphics Books.

> **Material:** short stories (wordless)
> **Genre:** horror
> **Age level:** middle school to adult
> **Language level:** all

Swiss graphic artist Thomas Ott is one of the reigning masters of the horror tale. He is also one of the most accomplished modern creators of wordless or mute comics, following in the footsteps of Frans Masereel (*Passionate Journey: A Novel in 165 Woodcuts*) and Lynd Ward (*The Silver Pony: A Story in Pictures*).

Dead End offers two tales done on scratchboard, with Ott's dense mesh of thin lines producing a dramatic and menacing play of light and shadow on every panel. In the first story, a suitcase full of money leads to an endless chain of murders. In the second, a hit man finds his "easy" mark, a midget magician, a lot harder to liquidate than anticipated. Ott's characters may reach a dead end, but his readers will find an open highway to chills and thrills.

The book's nine-by-twelve-inch format makes it big enough for a small-group read. Try the book with those students (and colleagues) who say they don't like horror stories. And then after they've read it for the third or fourth time, try to pry it out of their hands.

Flood! by Eric Drooker. 2002. Milwaukie, OR: Dark Horse Comics.

> **Material:** graphic novel (wordless)
> **Genre:** contemporary slice-of-life
> **Age level:** high school to adult
> **Language level:** all

Drooker's gorgeous images, done with a scratchboard technique similar to the layered crayon etching common in the primary grades, pull you into the book. The story those images tell keeps you there. An artist in New York City struggles with unemployment, homelessness, crime, and a crushing, relentless loneliness. His art promises an escape to a better life. Can pen and ink provide it?

Get those crayons ready! Once students see Drooker's artwork, they'll want to produce their own scratchboard stories.

Frank by Jim Woodring. 2000. Seattle, WA: Fantagraphics Books.

> **Material:** short stories (wordless)
> **Genre:** fantasy humor
> **Age level:** middle school to adult
> **Language level:** all

Woodring's bizarre imagery and abstruse story lines delight and bewilder in equal measure. Frank, who looks like he's part cat and part beaver with a touch of hippo, inhabits a universe where lighthouses are built in holes, giant hammers get angry, and fish are held for ransom. Frank makes you smile and three panels later gives you the chills. What this book won't do is bore your students. Everyone in the classroom will have an opinion about Frank. Consider having your rabid Frank Lovers debate your rabid Frank Haters.

GoGirl! by Trina Robbins and Anne Timmons. 2002. Milwaukie, OR: Dark Horse Comics. (See Figure 3–28a & b on pages 124 and 125.)

Material: graphic novel (collected comic book issues)
Genre: superheroine
Age level: middle school to high school
Language level: intermediate

When you're the only person at your high school who can fly, life gets interesting—and more than a little dangerous. Lindsay Goldman is the daughter of Go-Go Girl, a famous crime buster from the 1970s. She's inherited the maternal flying power and Mom's burning need to clobber the bad guys and right all wrongs. And that's just what she does, dressed in one of her mother's old costumes (complete with vinyl go-go boots) as GoGirl!, the teenage superheroine. Once GG flies into action, kidnappers, cattle rustlers, purse snatchers, bank robbers, and demon-possessed science teachers don't stand a chance. GoGirl! is a breath of fresh air for anyone weary of the superhero cliche: macho guy in tights defends helpless woman. In one story, Lindsay saves several school football players from certain death, including her current heartthrob, team star Dylan. But do superheroines really have time to date? Check the next installment of GoGirl!

Gon on Safari by Masashi Tanaka. 2000. New York: Paradox Press. (See Figure 3–7 on page 85.)

Material: short stories (wordless)
Genre: animal action adventure
Age level: primary to adult
Language level: all

In Gon, master illustrator Masashi Tanaka has done the near impossible: created a two-foot-tall dinosaur character whose appeal reaches from the primary grades through grad school. And all without a single word. Gon is about as far away from TV's cloying Barney as a dinosaur can get. This little guy is feisty, hot-tempered, and rough-and-tumble. Barney dances; Gon kicks butt. That scrappiness, however, is tempered by Gon's need to champion the underdog and protect the weak.

All the adventures in this and the other six Gon titles are set in present-day natural environments (African veldt, Antarctica, Australian Outback, American prairie, Siberian tundra), and feature indigenous animals, with no humans to muck up the works. How did Gon jump tens of millions of years into the present? Who knows? Just enjoy. This is picture storytelling at its best.

Grimmy: It's a Dog Sniff Dog World by Mike Peters. 2000. New York: Tom Doherty Associates. (See Figures 3–10 and 3–11 on page 94.)

> **Material:** comic strips
> **Genre:** humor
> **Age level:** grade 3 to adult
> **Language level:** early intermediate

Lovable dogs populate the comics. Satchel (Get Fuzzy), Odie (Garfield), Earl (Mutts), and Marmaduke may have their mischievous moments, but all are sweet pooches at heart. Bad-dog Grimmy provides some much-needed balance. How bad is he? In a typical week you'll find Grimmy drinking from the toilet bowl, taking his owner's car for a joyride, terrorizing the mail carrier and the meter maid, reading up on bird killing, and referring to cats as "the other white meat." Snoopy he ain't. Once your students have finished this volume and they're ready for more naughty dog adventures, try *Grimmy: The Postman Always Screams Twice!*

Peters sprinkles his strips with a number of pop culture references. For second language learners, the references increase the reading challenge and serve as catalysts for discussion and learning about important American icons.

Jar of Fools by Jason Lutes. 2001. Montreal: Drawn & Quarterly.

Material: graphic novel
Genre: contemporary slice-of-life
Age level: high school and adult
Language level: intermediate

Will Ernie, a hapless washed-up magician, ever get back on stage? Will Esther, the girlfriend who dumped him, quit her pushy new lover and the dead-end coffee shop job and ever come back? Will Flosso The Magnificient, Ernie's old show-biz mentor, be able to inspire and instruct his protégé again while struggling with senility? And finally, what about Nathan, single parent and irrepressible flimflam artist? Can he let go of petty crime long enough to raise that little daughter? For answers, dive into Lutes' crisp black and white drawings, where all these lives intersect in unexpected ways and where fools aren't nearly as foolish—or as uncaring—as they first appear.

I recently recommended *Jar of Fools* to an adult ed ESL teacher who was ready to give graphic novels a go but concerned that the text-spare books wouldn't have enough substance to them. She voiced the basic worry this way: "Do these things have enough story—enough meat—to talk and write about?" Her verdict on *Jar of Fools:* "Meaty!" Public librarian and author Steven Weiner (2001) included Lutes' book in his *The 101 Best Graphic Novels.*

The Last Lonely Saturday by Jordan Crane. 2000. Somerville, MA: Red Ink.

Material: graphic novel (mostly wordless)
Genre: contemporary slice-of-life
Age level: high school and adult
Language level: all

Each Saturday, a grieving widower visits the grave of his cherished Elenore, bringing flowers and seven new love letters. A surprise graveside visitor gives comfort, then a terrible scare, and a final release from heartache. Crane's "picto-novella" is a poignant musing on the power of love and memory, told in simple line drawings.

Many students will want to create a written story for the book or write and share their own personal stories of lost love. Keep a Kleenex box handy (Figure 4–5).

FIG. 4–5 *From* The Last Lonely Saturday *by
Jordan Crane. Copyright © 2000 by Jordan Crane.
Reprinted with permission of Reddingk,
.*

Monkey vs. Robot by James Kochalka. 2000. Marietta, GA: Top Shelf Productions.

Material: graphic novel (wordless)
Genre: action adventure
Age level: grade 3 to adult
Language level: all

Robots and toxic waste threaten a troop of monkeys and their forest home. Kochalka uses spare, two-tone drawings to spin an exciting—and violent—tale of battle between the natural and mechanized worlds. Who wins? Don't skip the epilogue! And don't miss the action-filled follow-up in the simian–metal men conflict *Monkey vs. Robot and the Crystal of Power.* The sequel has a light amount of text, appropriate for early intermediate students.

Pearls Before Swine: BLTs Taste So Darn Good by Stephan Pastis. 2003. Kansas City, MO: Andrews McMeel. (See Figure 2–5.)

Material: comic strips
Genre: humor
Age level: high school to adult
Language level: intermediate to advanced

A pretentious rat, a sweet but dim-bulb pig, a brainy goat, and a zebra obsessed with herd safety populate the Pearls Before Swine universe. The strip is a splendid blend of the philosophical, the sardonic, and the downright silly. This material works best with students who have intermediate to advanced English proficiency since many of the strips feature static and expressionless "talking heads." Such strips lack the visual clues that lower-proficient students rely on for meaning making. Even students with higher levels of English, however, will find some of the material a challenge. They'll need to dig into the dictionary, ask peers for help, and apply a host of reading comprehension strategies as they move through the text. Fortunately, students will do all that work without the teacher having to insist on it. Why? The jokes are that good.

By the way, if you like Satchel in Get Fuzzy, you'll like Pig in Pearls Before Swine. Pastis' Pig is every bit as good-natured as artist Darby Conley's loveable mutt—and just as slow on the uptake.

Persepolis by Marjane Satrapi. 2003. New York: Pantheon.

Material: graphic novel
Genre: memoir
Age level: high school and above
Language level: early advanced

Marjane Satrapi was only nine when the Islamic revolution shook Iran to its core in 1979. Rather than eliminate the repressions of the Shah's regime, however, the revolution continued and expanded them. Secular schools, coed schools, and bilingual education were outlawed. Universities were closed. Dissidents were tortured and executed. Soon, the "guardians of the revolution" had labeled a bewildering array of items as "decadent," including jeans, jewelry, alcohol, parties, rock music, dancing, card games, and chess. The veil became obligatory. At the same time, the long and bitter war with Iraq made life even more perilous for Marjane, her family, and all Iranians. At one point in the story, Marjane's uncle, imprisoned by the Shah and later executed by the Islamic Republic, implores that "Our family memory must not be lost." Ms. Satrapi's raw and unblinking autobiography guarantees that memory a long life.

Persepolis will inspire many students to mine their own family histories for tales worth remembering. The logical next step in the classroom: committing the tales to paper—and to memory—with drawings and text.

Road to Perdition by Max Allan Collins and Richard Piers Rayner. 1998. New York: Paradox Press.

Material: graphic novel
Genre: crime drama
Age level: middle school and above
Language level: intermediate

A young boy witnesses a shocking crime and is suddenly caught up in a world of Depression-era gangsters, robbery, betrayal, and revenge. The boy's only hope for survival is the protection offered by his father, a legendary mob enforcer known as the "Archangel of Death." Can the Angel get his son to a safe house in Perdition, Kansas, before the Capone mob nail them both? Students will be turning pages faster than a machine gun spits lead to find out. The writing is crisp and the richly detailed pictures pull the reader straight into the rough-and-tumble times of early 1930s America. Students bitten by the mystery-thriller bug will want to read other titles from the Paradox Graphic Mystery series as well as Martin Mysteries from Dark Horse Comics.

Sshhhh! by Jason. 2002. Seattle, WA: Fantagraphics Books.

> **Material:** graphic novel (wordless)
> **Genre:** contemporary slice-of-life
> **Age level:** high school to adult
> **Language level:** all

A beak-heavy crow who sports a flashy jacket and a fedora is run through the emotional ringer in *Sshhhh!* Crow endures boredom, loneliness, child-parent separation, and lost love. Life as a tin-whistle-playing street musician is never easy, but Crow's biggest battle is with "the devils" inside: his jealousy, anger, and remorse. Ultimately, Crow triumphs. He's a survivor, though true happiness remains elusive.

This book is a challenging, thought-provoking read. Many students will want—and need—to read it with a partner for discussion and meaning making. Jason's pictures provide the base for dialogue writing and plenty of caption description, including time and setting changes, character background information, and off-panel action.

The System by Peter Kuper. 1997. New York: DC Comics.

> **Material:** graphic novel (wordless)
> **Genre:** crime drama
> **Age level:** high school and above
> **Language level:** all

Kuper populates this wordless novel with a dizzying array of characters, including a washed up detective, stripper-mom, corporate hustler, sidewalk preacher, crooked cop, and an assortment of graffiti artists, ill-fated lovers, and gangbangers. And then to make things really interesting, the artist throws in a serial killer and a bomb-making terrorist. Confusing? Not with Kuper's extraordinary talent for graphic storytelling. Each character thread is woven into a coherent and satisfying whole. Disparate lives intersect and are transformed in this compelling look at the struggles, dreams, disappointments, and terrors of many urban dwellers.

The System is equal parts crime thriller and social criticism, and a page-turner from start to finish. Be careful, however, how fast those pages turn. If you've got students who are new to this genre of comic, you may find them zooming through *The System's* hundred and five pages in four or five minutes. The novel merits—and requires—a good forty to sixty minutes. My gentle, but straightforward reminder for all the zoomers: Slow down. Read the pictures. Enjoy.

Trenches by Scott Mills. 2002. Marietta, GA: Top Shelf Productions.

> **Material:** graphic novel
> **Genre:** historical fiction
> **Age level:** high school to adult
> **Language level:** early intermediate

Two brothers from England endure the hardships and horrors of World War I France. Only one returns home. Mills uses spare black and white drawings and equally lean dialogue to convey the terrible realities of trench warfare: lice, mud, boredom, deafening noise, poison gas, and the ever present twin terrors of No Man's Land, fear and death (Figure 4–6).

If your language target is American English, the Britishisms in the novel may deter you. But I hope not. Take the plunge and you'll find an exciting and touching tale plus some interesting lexical variations for contrasting how English is spoken in different parts of the world.

WJHC: On the Air! by Jane Smith Fisher. 2003. Oceanside, NY: Wilson Place Comics.

> **Material:** graphic novel (collected comic book issues)
> **Genre:** teen adventure
> **Age level:** middle school and high school
> **Language level:** intermediate

FIG. 4–6 *From* Trenches *by Scott Mills. Copyright © 2002 by Scott Mills. Reprinted by permission of Top Shelf Productions, Inc.,* <www.topshelfcomix.com/>.

Music fills the halls at Jackson Hill High each morning. A great way for students to start the day, right? Not when kids want hard rock and the school insists on dental-office light. Fed up with the daily musical torment, teen go-getter Janey Wells and her buddies launch radio station WJHC. The Jackson Hill crowd includes The Skate, the coolest DJ since Wolfman Jack; Roland Drayton, WJHC's electronically challenged chief engineer; Tara O'Toole, rich kid know-it-all; Ciel Chin-King, bright idea gal; and Sandy Diaz, a Mr. Fix-It who's hopelessly lovesick over Janey. After reading about all the fun and action at WJHC, some of your second language learners may want to work in pairs or small groups and write and record short radio programs. You may need a can-do student like Janey Wells, however, to get any airplay during schoolwide morning announcements! (See Figures 4–7a, 4–7b.)

The Yellow Jar: Two Tales from Japanese Tradition by Patrick Atangan. 2002. New York: NBM.

Material: short stories
Genre: folktale
Age level: middle school and above
Language level: early advanced

Atangan spins two stories of devotion, courage, and triumph with gorgeous pictures drawn in the style of 18th century Japanese woodblock prints. In the first tale, a poor fisherman finds a large yellow jar floating in the sea. Inside is O Haru San, a lovely maiden searching the world for a suitable mate. They fall in love and marry, but their happiness is soon undone by the fisherman's one small betrayal. The woman returns to the sea in her yellow jar and is taken prisoner by Hoso No Kami, the demon warrior. O Haru San is faced with a terrible dilemma: marry the demon or kill herself. Time is running out. The fisherman must quickly locate his wife, win back her trust, and defeat the most powerful fighter in the land before all is lost.

In the second tale, two weed-maidens take root in the Empire's most beautiful garden. The garden is tended by Issa, a humble monk who tries everything in his power to force the weeds to leave. They refuse to budge and then suddenly blossom into gorgeous chrysanthemums, one yellow and one white. Issa laments his foolishness and lavishes attention on the two beauties. Another Ugly Duckling story? Not quite. Local villagers detect a slight flaw in the white mum, and the monk's preferential treatment for the perfect yellow flower leads to danger—and an important life lesson.

A logical next step for students who enjoy the *Yellow Jar*: creating comics based on favorite folktales from their home countries.

FIG. 4–7a *From* WJHC: On the Air! *By Jane Smith Fisher. Copyright © 2003 by Jane Smith Fisher. Reprinted by permission of Wilson Place Comics, Inc.,* <www.wjhc.com/>.

FIG. 4–7b *From* WJHC: On the Air! *By Jane Smith Fisher. Copyright © 2003 by Jane Smith Fisher. Reprinted by permission of Wilson Place Comics, Inc., <www.wjhc.com/>.*

Online Reviews

I often get comics requests from teachers and students. They may be looking for a specific type of comic or have a title in mind and are wondering about content and quality. Over the past year or so, requests have included:

- a story about 1960s pop music (*Days Like This*)
- the conflict in Bosnia (*Fax from Sarajevo*)
- Cervantes' Don Quixote for struggling L2 readers (*The Last Knight*)
- a sci-fi adventure with an environmental message and a strong female lead (*Nausicaa of the Valley of the Wind*)
- an African American teen superhero (*Static Shock: Trial by Fire*)
- something done in a gangster-detective film noir style (*Torso*)

Sometimes I can quickly come up with a title and some helpful information; many times I can't. When I strike out, I turn to the following resources for title possibilities and reviews:

Beek's Books: *www.rzero.com/books/index.html*
Dozens of insightful reviews across several genres, with sample panels.

Berkeley Public Library:
www.infopeople.org/bpl/teen/graphic.html
Short descriptions of graphic novels.

Bob's Comics Reviews: *www.zompist.com/bob.shtml*
Thoughtful, in-depth reviews of selected graphic novels and comic strips.

Dawn Imada's Reviews:
www.geocities.com/dawnanik/grnovels.htm
Recommendations (with short descriptions) of graphic novels and comic trade paperbacks by Dawn Imada, a young adult services librarian, from the San Jose Public Library System, San Jose, California.

Diamond Bookshelf Reviews:

bookshelf.diamondcomics.com/reviews/
Monthly reviews by librarian Katharine Kan.

No Flying No Tights:

The three-woman team at No Flying No Tights maintains three of the best comics review sites on the Web.

Site 1: For kids (Sidekicks):

sidekicks.noflyingnotights.com/
Each graphic novel reviewed includes a picture of the cover. Genres: superheroes, fantasy, sci-fi, mystery, action and adventure, humor, realism, and nonfiction.

Site 2: For teens (the original No Flying No Tights site):

www.noflyingnotights.com/index2.html
All the genres at the kiddie site, plus: historical fiction, crime and suspense, romance, and horror.

Site 3: For teens and adults (The Lair):

lair.noflyingnotights.com/

Steve Raiteri's Graphic Novel Reviews:

my.voyager.net/~sraiteri/graphicnovels.htm
A wide-ranging selection of reviews. Steve is a librarian for the Greene County Public Library in Xenia, Ohio, and reviews graphic novels bimonthly for *Library Journal.*

Online Comics

It's a big comics world, but to find it we've got to venture beyond the handful of cartoons and strips appearing in our local newspaper. For additional comics for the activities in this book—and for pure reading enjoyment!—try the following sites. You'll find hundreds and hundreds of comics with a vast range of topics, styles, and text loads.

Directory Sites (large repositories):

Comics.com: *www.comics.com/*
ComicsPage.com: *www.comicspage.com/index.htm*

King Features: *www.kingfeatures.com/features/comics/comics.htm*
OnlineComics.net: *www.onlinecomics.net/index.php*
    At last count: 2,650 comics in sixteen categories!
phpGrabComics: *www.baravalle.it/phpGrabComics/index.php*
Stu's Comic Strip Connection: *www.stus.com/index2.htm*
uComics: *www.ucomics.com/*
WebComics: *www.webcomics.com/*

Editorial Cartoons

Daryl Cagle's Professional Cartoonists Index

   cagle.slate.msn.com/

This site contains a vast number of archived editorial cartoons from
around the world. Plug a topic into the search box and you'll quickly
locate what you need. Be sure to visit the Teacher Guide section. Five
new editorial cartoons are highlighted each week and include essential background information, student discussion questions, and links
to relevant websites. A goldmine.

    For more cartoons, check the editorial cartoon section at
Comics.Com at <*www.comics.com/*> and at UComics.com at
<*www.ucomics.com/*>.

Comic Books and Graphic Novels

Here's a selection of sites where students can read complete, multi-
page comics.

ACTION ADVENTURE

EHA Comics: *www.ehacomics.com/*
INARI: *knotwood.netfirms.com/comics.htm*
The Jaded: *thejaded.keenspace.com/*
Mikka Adventures (manga): *cyyeun.xepher.net/manga.htm*

CRIME DRAMA

Grave Digger: *www.atomicpulp.com/main.html*
Night Warrior: *www.nw-comic.co.uk/*

DRAMA/SLICE-OF-LIFE

City Yarns: *www.cityyarns.com/*
Consumed: *www.gozers.com/*
The Way to Your Heart (manga): *www.emi-art.com/twtyh/main.html*

FANTASY

Aelyf the Scribe: *www.lairdogden.com/*
Falcon Twin (manga): *www.falcontwin.com/*
Keepers of the Forest: *keepersoftheforestcomics.com/Page_1x.html*
Sevenplains: *mentaltentacle.com/*
Tomb of the King: *keepersoftheforestcomics.com/Page_1x.html*

HORROR

Elsie Hooper: *www.elsiehooper.com/*
Menace from the Marsh: *resolutes.keenspace.com/archive.html*
Statuette of Madness: *www.pedrolopez.dk/*
Zombie Hunter: *www.zombiehunter.com/*

MYSTERY/SUSPENSE

The Compleat Alice: *alice.xepher.net/*
Femme Noir: *www.supernaturalcrime.com/*
Grand Blue Door: *www.grandbluedoor.com/*

ROMANCE

Another Date: *studiocyen.net/comics/another/*
A Chinese Ghost Story:
 www.fortunecity.com/westwood/indigo/322/acgs/acgs-manga.html
Down But Not Out: *studiocyen.net/comics/failed/*
Red String (manga): *redstring.strawberrycomics.com/*

SCI-FI

Ghosthunters: *www.ghosthunterscomics.com/*
Post-Nuke: *www.postnukecomic.com/*
The Price of Your Skin: *www.angelfire.com/comics/pinton/skin01.html*
Terinu: *www.terinu.net/*

SUPERHERO/SUPERHEROINE

Calling All Heroes!: *resolutes.keenspace.com/archive.html*
Canadiana: *www.sandycarruthers.com/*
Dasien: *www.drunkduck.com/Dasien/*
The League of Space Captains: *resolutes.keenspace.com/archive.html*
Tales of the Tower Raven:
 www.angelfire.com/comics/red_bee/towerraven.html

VARIOUS (multiple genres)

ModernTales (some free plus by subscription):
 www.moderntales.com/
PV Comics (some free plus by subscription): *www.pvcomics.com/*

Special Interests

In the vast world of comics, there's a title to match nearly any student or teacher interest. Here's a small sampling of "specialty" items, mostly humorous comic strips, arranged alphabetically by category.

African American (featured characters)

The Boondocks (humor/political):   *www.ucomics.com/*
Curtis (humor):   *www.kingfeatures.com/*
Herb and Jamaal (humor):   *www.Creators.com/comics.html*
Housebroken (humor):   *www.ucomics.com/*
Jump Start (humor):   *www.comics.com/*
Mama's Boyz (humor):   *www.mamasboyz.com/intro.html*

Animal (all humor)

Bob the Squirrel: *www.bobthesquirrel.com/index.html*
Heathcliff: *www.comics.com/*
Pearls Before Swine: *www.comics.com/*
Spot the Frog: *www.comics.com/*
Webbster & Button: *www.alachuahumane.org/comics/*

Asian American (featured characters)

American Born Chinese (slice-of-life stories):
   www.moderntales.com/
Angry Little Girls! (humor):   *angrylittlegirls.com/*
Badmash (humor/South Asian):   *www.badmash.org/*

Business, Industry, and Technology (all humor)

Bull$ 'N' Bear$:   *www.comics.com/*
CEO Dad: *www.comics.com/*
Fat Cats: *www.comics.com/*
PC and Pixel: *www.comics.com/*

Continuity Strips (serials)

Alley Oop (adventure):   *www.comics.com/comics/alleyoop/index.html*
Annie (Little Orphan Annie) (drama/adventure):
   www.comicspage.com/index.html
Brenda Starr (adventure/romance):   *www.ucomics.com/*
Dick Tracy (crime):   *www.ucomics.com/*
For Better or For Worse (slice-of-life):   *www.comics.com/*
Luann (humor):   *www.comics.com/*
The Phantom (action adventure):   *www.kingfeatures.com/*

Prince Valiant (action adventure/historical):   *www.kingfeatures.com/*
(The Amazing) Spider-Man (action adventure):
   www.kingfeatures.com/
Tarzan (adventure):   *www.comics.com/*

Family Fare (all humor)
Baby Blues: *www.kingfeatures.com/*
Committed: *www.comics.com/*
Drabble: *www.comics.com/*
Get Fuzzy: *www.comics.com/*
Grand Avenue: *www.comics.com/*

Gay/Lesbian (featured characters)
Adam & Andy (slice-of-life):   *www.adamandandy.com/*
Honestly Ethel (slice-of-life):   *www.comicazee.com/cartoonist.asp?id=2*
Jane's World (slice-of-life):
   www.comics.com/comics/janesworld/index.html
Lady Blue (set in pre-war Germany):
   archive.salon.com/comics/dark/2/lady/1999/02/19lady1.html

Kids and Teens (featured characters)
Archie Comics: *www.archiecomics.com/comic_shop/comic_shop.html*
Archie (the strip):   *www.Creators.com/comics.html*
FoxTrot: *www.ucomics.com/*
Peanuts: *www.comics.com/*
Preteena: *www.ucomics.com/*
Rugrats: *www.Creators.com/comics.html*
Wee Pals: *www.Creators.com/comics.html*
Zits: *www.kingfeatures.com/*

Latino (featured characters)
Baldo (humor):   *www.ucomics.com/*
La Cucaracha (humor):   *www.ucomics.com/*

Law/Medical Professions (cartoons)
Stu's Views: *www.stus.com/index.htm*

Native American (featured characters)
Blue Corn Comics (Peace Party comic books):
   www.bluecorncomics.com/

Religious

Amar Chitra Katha (Immortal Picture Stories) (Hindu) (order only):
  www.navrang.com/index.php

Church Mice (Christian): *www.zorowski.com/churchmice*

Dharma the Cat (Buddhist): *www.dharmathecat.com/*

ICNA (Islamic Circle of North America):
  www.icna.org/youth/comics.htm

Yossie & Co. (Jewish): *www.ohr.org.il/yossi/*

Science/Math

The Periodic Table of Comic Books:
  www.uky.edu/Projects/Chemcomics/index.html

From faculty in the Department of Chemistry, University of Kentucky.
  Amazing! This was the site I needed when I took high school
  chemistry!

Webcomics Lessons for Algebra Students (Gene Yang):
  www.geocities.com/misteryang/factoring/index.html

Sports

Cleats (soccer): *www.ucomics.com/*

Gil Thorp (various): *www.ucomics.com/*

In the Bleachers (various): *www.ucomics.com/*

Tank McNamara (various): *www.ucomics.com/*

Student-Made Comics

Amazing Kids (nonprofit educational organization):
  www.amazing-kids.org/index.html
  Lots of comic strips done by students ages six to seventeen. Click
  on "AK Comics."

Camino Union School District (California): *www.camino.k12.ca.us/*
  Grade 8 comic strip projects. Includes both hand-drawn roughs
  and computer-assisted finished strips.

Canby School District (Canby, Oregon):
  wigowsky.topcities.com/Egypt/book/books.htm
  Grade 6 comic book projects on Egypt.

Dubuque Community School District (Dubuque, Iowa):
  www.dubuque.k12.ia.us/Fulton/Cartoon_Club/cartoonists/

Student comics done in Jeff Dyer's Cartoon Club at Fulton School. Jeff is an elementary teacher and professional cartoonist.

Silver Star School (Vernon, B.C., Canada):
www.sd22.bc.ca/silverstar/writing/writing.html
Grade 7 superhero-based comic books.

Women/Girls (featured characters)
Humor strips at Comics.com: *www.comics.com/*
    Agnes
    Flo & Friends
    Momma
    Rose Is Rose

Humor strips at uComics.com: *www.ucomics.com/*
    Cathy
    Helen, Sweetheart of the Internet
    Lola
    Sylvia

Comics in Other Languages

Arabic
Disney Comics: *www.angelfire.com/comics/disney/index.html*

Chinese
Taiwanimation Online (various):
    taiwanimation.tripod.com/comics.html

Dutch
Billy Biever (strips, comic adventures of a beaver): *www.billybiever.nl/*

French
BD Paradisio (various): *www.bdparadisio.com/*

German
Akte Nix (German) (strips, adventure/sci-fi):
    home.t-online.de/home/bischoff-mail/
ByteComics (German comics directory):
    bytecomics.de/verzeichnis/?kid=800

Hebrew

Golem: *www.multiverse.co.il/kaboom/golem/golem.html*

Indonesian (various strips)

indiecomic.endonesa.net/index.htm

Italian

Diabolik (crime drama):   *www.diabolik.it/*

Japanese

Mangarama (Japanese as a second language with audio):
www.ak.cradle.titech.ac.jp/Rise/top.htm

Russian

GrimJim (humor/adventure strips and comic books)
www.grimjim.com.ua/new.php
LearningRussian.com: *learningrussian.com/comics/index.htm*

Spanish

A number of well-known English language strips are available in Spanish.
At King Features (*www.king-online.com/main/features.php3*) you'll find:

Baby Blues
Barney Google & Snuffy Smith
Beetle Bailey
Blondie
Buckles
Crock
Hägar the Horrible
Hi and Lois
Marvin
Mutts
Phantom
Piranha Club
Sherman's Lagoon
Spanish Spiderman
Spanish Zits

At uComics.com (*www.ucomics.com/*) you'll find:

Baldo
Calvin and Hobbes

Cathy
FoxTrot
Fred Basset
Garfield
Modesty Blaise
Pooch Café
Ziggy

Aftercomic (adventure, humor, and slice-of-life):
   www.aftercomic.com/content.htm
Batcan (superhero parody):   *www.virtuacomics.8k.com/batcan1.html*
Camulus (fifth-century adventure):   *www.camulusweb.com.ar/*
El Capitán Pantera (humor/adventure):
   www.delcomic.es/carr/inicio.htm
Fontanarrosa (cartoon):   *www.baravalle.it/phpGrabComics/index.php*
Historias Espaciales (sci-fi/humor strip):
   www.historiasespaciales.com.ar/
Riolfo Veridela (sci-fi adventure):
   www.geocities.com/riolfoveridela/main.html
Tierra Antigua (graphic novel–horror/macabre):
   www.creativoides.com/Novgra.html
Tiras Cómicas (humor strips, including Peanuts, Calvin and Hobbes):
   jubilo.ca/tiras/

Swahili
Sasa Sema Publications (by order):   *www.sasasema.com/index.html*

Swedish
Lila DeLila (superheroine adventure):
   home.swipnet.se/~w-27161/svensk.html
Mammas Gata (humor strip):
   www.mammasgata.com/cgi-bin/autokeenlite.cgi

Tagalog
Pugad Baboy (humor strip):   *www.pmjunior.com.ph/*

Multiple Languages
Archie Comics: *www.archiecomics.com/comic_shop/comic_shop.html*
In Spanish, French, Greek, Norwegian, Swedish, German, and
   Korean. Complete comic books. Click on shelf marked "Foreign
   Language Comics."

Disney Comics: *www.donaldisten.dk/comics/*
    In English, Dutch, Arabic, Norwegian, Finnish, Italian.
European Comics on the Web:
    lcg-www.uia.ac.be/~erikt/comics/welcome.html

Other Resources

Censorship Issues

If you ever have a comic challenged by a parent or administrator, the following organizations offer a variety of censorship-fighting resources.

American Library Association (Office for Intellectual Freedom)
    www.ala.org/Template.cfm?Section=oif
Comic Book Legal Defense Fund   *www.cbldf.org/index.shtml*

Comic Shop Locator

To find the nearest comic book shop:
Online at <*csls.diamondcomics.com/*>. Phone: 1-888-266–4226 (toll free)

Comics Conventions

Wondering if there's a comics convention near you anytime soon? Check the Convention Calendar at *www.comicbookconventions.com/*.

Comics-Film Connection

Some students come to reading through film, a Batman movie, for example, spurring interest in Batman comics and the comics, in turn, stimulating interest in other reading materials. For your student film fans, here's a list of movies based on popular comics. All are available on DVD. The list is far from exhaustive. For more comics-inspired films and their release dates, consult Comics2Film at *www.comics2film.com/*.

    Akira (2001, animated)
    Barefoot Gen (1992, animated)
    Batman (1989)
    Batman Returns (1992)
    Batman: Mask of the Phantasm (1993, animated)
    Blade (1998)
    Blade II (2002)

Conan the Barbarian (1982)
The Crow (1994)
Daredevil (2003)
Dick Tracy (1990)
From Hell (2001)
Ghost World (2001)
Hellboy (2004)
Hulk (2003)
The League of Extraordinary Gentleman (2003)
Road to Perdition (2002)
The Phantom (1996)
The Punisher (1989; 2004)
Sheena (1984)
Spawn (1997)
Spider-Man (2002)
Spider-Man2 (2004)
Supergirl (1984)
Superman: The Movie (1978)
Superman II (1981)
Tales from the Crypt Presents Demon Night (1995)
Tarzan (1999, animated)
X-Men (2000)
X2: X-Men United (2003)

ANIME (Japanese animation films)

Huge numbers of anime are based on Japanese comics (manga) titles. Many of these films are redubbed or subtitled for export to English-speaking countries. For a frequently updated list of available titles, check Steve Raiteri's webpage at *www.koyagi.com/AM.html*.

COMICS FOR SOCIAL CHANGE

www.worldcomics.fi/wcmxmain.html

Groups and individuals around the world use comics to promote a variety of social justice issues, including human rights, immigrant rights, gender equity, and health care. You'll find examples from several different countries plus helpful hints on how to create and launch your own "comics campaign." For more samples and how-to ideas, see *<global.finland.fi/comics/>*. This site features an Internet edition of

Comics with an Attitude: A Guide to the Use of Comics in Development Information, by Leif Packalén (Finland) and Frank Odoi (Ghana).

COMICS PUBLISHERS

AiT/PlanetLar (graphic novels): *www.astronautsintrouble.com/*

Antarctic Press (American manga): *www.antarctic-press.com/*

Archie Comics (Archie, Betty & Veronica, and the whole Riverdale gang): *www.archiecomics.com/*

CPM Manga (manga):
www.centralparkmedia.com/cpmcomics/cpmcomic.htm

CrossGeneration Comics (fantasy and sci-fi): *www.crossgen.com/*

Dark Horse Comics (multiple genres): *www.dhorse.com/*

DC Comics (multiple genres): *www.dccomics.com/*
For: Batman, Batgirl, Green Lantern, Hawkman, JLA (Justice League of America), Looney Tunes, Plastic Man, Superman, Wonder Woman

Fantagraphics (multiple genres): *www.fantagraphics.com/*
For: Astro Boy, Bone, Frank, Love & Rockets, Popeye, Prince Valiant, Tintin, Usagi Yojimbo, Zippy

Gemstone Publishing (Disney comics): *www.gemstonepub.com/*
Disney comics are back! Reprints of Disney comics featuring classic favorites like Uncle Scrooge, Mickey Mouse, Minnie Mouse, Goofy, Donald Duck

Marvel: *www.marvel.com/flash.htm*
For: Spider-Man, Spider-Girl, X-Men, Captain America, Incredible Hulk, Elektra, Thor, Daredevil, Iron Man

Paradox Press (multiple genres): *www.dccomics.com/paradox/*

TokyoPop (manga): *www.tokyopop.com/*
For: Chobits, CLAMP School Detectives, Ice Blade, Princess Ai, Sailor Moon, Warriors of Tao

VIZ (manga): *www.viz.com/*
For: Ceres (Celestial Legend), Dragon Ball Z, INUYASHA, Naruto, Ranma 1/2, Tenchi Muyo, X/1999

How-to-Draw Resources

Here are some resources for those students—and teachers—wanting to move beyond flat, static, stick-figure drawings. They won't turn anyone into a syndicated cartoonist overnight, but they'll help you add two essential ingredients to your comics: depth and movement.

HOW-TO-DRAW BOOKS

Cartooning Basics by Duane Barnhart. 1997. White Bear Lake, MN: Cartoon Connections Press.

Draw 3-D: A Step-by-Step Guide to Perspective Drawing by Doug DuBosque. 1999. Columbus, NC: Peel Productions.

Draw Alien Fantasies by Damon J. Reinagle. 1996. Columbus, NC: Peel Productions.
Other great books in the Draw series by Doug DuBosque, Damon Reinagle (all available through Peel Productions Inc., Columbus, North Carolina).

- *Draw Cars*
- *Draw Sports Figures*
- *Draw Insects*
- *Draw Grassland Animals*
- *Draw Rainforest Animals*
- *Draw Ocean Animals*
- *Draw Dinosaurs*

Drawing Dynamic Comics by Andy Smith. 2000. New York: Watson-Guptill.

Draw Your Own Cartoons by Don Mayne. 2000. Charlotte, VT: Williamson.

Manga Mania: How to Draw Japanese Comics by Christopher Hart. 2000. New York: Watson-Guptill.

Toons! How to Draw Wild and Lively Characters for All Kinds of Cartoons by Randy Glasbergen. 1997. Cincinnati, OH: North Light Books.

HOW-TO-DRAW WEBSITES

Create a Creature (for kids and teens):
www.afordturtle.com.cnchost.com/CreateACreature/index.html
Step-by-step creature/monster drawings from Aaron Riddle, who draws the Aford (the turtle) strip.

Draw and Color with Uncle Fred (for primary-grade kids):
www.unclefred.com/
Very basic, step-by-step, near foolproof cartooning.

Fundoodle.com (for primary-grade kids):
www.fundoodle.com/fundrawing.asp
Draw a boy, girl, and lots of animals (dog, duck, lion, mouse, pig, squirrel), each in five easy steps.

Poveytoons.com (for kids and teens):
www.btinternet.com/~william.povey/
Learn to draw characters from William Mark Povey's Albert Duck comic strip.

Slylock Fox & Comics for Kids (for kids and teens):
www.slylockfox.com/
Step-by-step help with lots of wonderful drawings. The "Cow" and the "Puppy with a Pizza" are my favorites.

Epilogue

few weeks before completing the book, I had two notable comics-related encounters. The first reminds us that going graphic in some schools is still an uphill struggle; the second, why we need to keep climbing the hill.

Passing Up the Freebies

One Saturday afternoon I was rummaging through used titles at my neighborhood comics shop and struck up a conversation with a fellow "bin-diver." We both had some gray in our hair, and it's always fun talking with someone who read the same comics I read as a kid. After a few minutes of reminiscing, the man told me he'd recently culled through his vast collection and pulled out a number of duplicate and unwanted items. He'd sorted and boxed up all the comics, then called the librarian at a nearby high school and offered her the lot for free.

The man had read about the school's money woes and its need for more library materials, and thought donating the comics might be one small, but still important way to "do his bit" and help. He would deliver the comics straight to the school and didn't need a tax receipt. Here were free and easy materials for the taking.

The librarian said thanks, but no thanks. There might be inappropriate content in some of the items and besides, this was school and students read books at school, not comics. "Can you believe it?" the man asked me. "Over three hundred comics and the school wouldn't take them!" I believed it.

More Comics, More English

A couple days later I was back on the consulting trail, preparing for a comics-based workshop for a school district in the San Francisco Bay Area. I needed thirty-five teacher handouts and headed to my local copy shop and dropped off the master packet. The young clerk who waited on me was a recent immigrant from Bosnia. I'd spoken briefly with him on previous visits, complimented him on his excellent English, and had learned the copy job was only temporary till he found work in his chosen field of study—computer science.

In times past, I was always in and out of the shop in under three minutes. Submit the packet, give the copying instructions, and away I went. Not today. I was nearly out the door when the clerk spotted the comics in the packet and called me back to the counter. "You use the comics with the teachers?" he asked, pointing to the school district's name on the cover page. When I said I did and that I also used them with students, he broke into a huge smile and excitedly proclaimed, "This is wonderful! I use the comics for me!"

We talked comics for close to forty minutes, right through his scheduled coffee break. The young man stated he'd learned most of his English by watching American films and reading lots and lots of comics. He used films and comics in Bosnia for English development and was still using them in the United States. I asked if comics had been a part of his formal English studies in school, either at home or in his ESL classes in this country. Nope. If they had, he assured me, "I know more English now!" He was delighted—but astonished—to find an educator who not only read comics but actually used them in schools. Before I left the shop, the young man wrote out a long list of the "best good comics in English!" and asked me to please recommend the titles in my workshop. I promised him I would and continue to share his list with interested teachers.

* * *

Thanks for joining me on the flight through Comics Land. I hope you spotted something along the way—a theoretical principle, study, strategy, or activity—that sparked your interest. I wish you every success in putting comics to work in your multilingual classroom. Up, up, and away!

References

Ada, A. F. 1988. "The Pajaro Valley Experience: Working with Spanish-Speaking Parents to Develop Children's Reading and Writing Skills in the Home Through the Use of Children's Literature." In *Minority Education: From Shame to Struggle*, edited by T. Skutnabb-Kangas and J. Cummins. Clevedon, England: Multilingual Matters.

American Library Association. The 100 Most Frequently Challenged Books of 1990–2000. Accessed at *www.ala.org/ala/oif/bannedbooksweek/bbwlinks/100mostfrequently.htm*.

Anderson, R. C., and P. D. Pearson. 1984. "A Schema-Theoretic View of Basic Processes in Reading." In *Handbook of Reading Research*, edited by P. D. Pearson. White Plains, NY: Longman.

Anderson, R. C., P. T. Wilson, and L. G. Fielding. 1988. "Growth in Reading and How Children Spend Their Time Outside of School." *Reading Research Quarterly* 23 (summer): 285–303.

Armstrong, T. 2000. *Multiple Intelligences in the Classroom*. 2d ed. Alexandria, VA: Association for Supervision and Curriculum Development.

———. 2003. *The Multiple Intelligences of Reading and Writing: Making the Words Come Alive*. Alexandria, VA: Association for Supervision and Curriculum Development.

"Better Retailing: Expanding Your Sales to Women." 2001. An ICv2.com interview with Joe Ferrara of Atlantis Fantasyworld, Santa Cruz, California. Accessed at *www.icv2.com/articles/indepth/683.html.*

Black, K. 1991. "How Students See Their Writing: A Visual Representation of Literacy." *Journal of Reading* 35 (3): 206–14.

Brown, H. D. 2000. *Principles of Language Learning and Teaching.* 4th ed. White Plains, NY: Longman.

"Cage Sells Comics Collection." *St. Petersburg Times.* 2002. Accessed at *www.sptimes.com/2002/10/15/Artsandentertainment/In_the_news.shtml.*

Caine, R. N., and G. Caine. 1997. *Education on the Edge of Possibility.* Alexandria, VA: Association for Supervision and Curriculum Development.

Carter, C. J. 1997. "Why Reciprocal Teaching?" *Educational Leadership* 54 (6): 64–68.

Cary, S. 1998. The Effectiveness of a Contextualized Storytelling Approach for Second Language Acquisition. Doctoral dissertation, University of San Francisco, San Francisco, California.

Celce-Murcia, M., and E. Olshtain. 2000. *Discourse and Context in Language Teaching: A Guide for Language Teachers.* Cambridge: Cambridge University Press.

Chamot, A. U., and J. M. O'Malley. 1994. *The CALLA Handbook: Implementing the Cognitive Academic Language Learning Approach.* Reading, MA: Addison-Wesley.

Chilcoat, G.W. 1993. "Teaching About the Civil Rights Movement by Using Student-Generated Comic Books." *The Social Studies* 84 (May/June): 113–18.

Chilcoat, G. W., and J. Ligon. 1994. "The Underground Comix: A Popular Culture Approach to Teaching Historical, Political, and Social Issues of the Sixties and Seventies." *Michigan Social Studies Journal* 7 (fall): 35–40.

Dorrell, L., and E. Carroll. 1981. "Spider-Man at the Library." *School Library Journal* 27 (August): 17–19.

Dorrell, L. D., D. B. Curtis, and K. R. Rampal. 1995. "Book-Worms Without Books? Students Reading Comic Books in the School House." *Journal of Popular Culture* 29 (fall): 223–34.

Dulay, H., M. Burt, and S. Krashen. 1982. *Language Two.* New York: Oxford University Press.

Edelsky, C., B. Altwerger, and B. Flores. 1991. *Whole Language: What's the Difference?* Portsmouth, NH: Heinemann.

Eisner, W. 1985. *Comics and Sequential Art.* Tamarac, FL: Poorhouse Press.

Elley, W. B. 1991. "Acquiring Literacy in a Second Language: The Effect of Book-Based Programs." *Language Learning* 41 (3): 375–411.

Flurkey, A. D., and J. Xu. eds. 2003. *On the Revolution of Reading: The Selected Writings of Kenneth S. Goodman.* Portsmouth, NH: Heinemann.

Fountas, I. C., and G. S. Pinnell. 2001. *Guiding Readers and Writers Grades 3–6: Teaching Comprehension, Genre, and Content Literacy.* Portsmouth, NH: Heinemann.

Freeman, D. E., and Y. S. Freeman. 2001. *Between Worlds: Access to Second Language Acquisition.* 2d ed. Portsmouth, NH: Heinemann.

Freire, P. 1970. *Pedagogy of the Oppressed.* New York: The Continuum.

Gardner, H. 1983. *Frames of Mind: The Theory of Multiple Intelligences.* New York: Basic Books.

Gardner, R. C., and W. E. Lambert. 1972. *Attitudes and Motivation in Second-Language Learning.* Rowley, MA: Newbury House.

Goodman, K. 1986. *What's Whole in Whole Language?* Portsmouth, NH: Heinemann.

Graves, D. 2002. *Testing Is Not Teaching: What Should Count in Education.* Portsmouth, NH: Heinemann.

Hart, L. A. 1983. *Human Brain and Human Learning.* Village of Oak Creek, AZ: Books for Educators.

Hatch, E. 1992. *Discourse and Language Education.* Cambridge: Cambridge University Press.

"Hey Kids, a New Holiday!" 2003. Beth Negus Viveiros. Direct (Direct Marketing Business Intelligence). Accessed at *www.directmag.com/ar/marketing_hey_kids _new/*.

Holmes, V. L., and M. R. Moulton. 1994. "The Writing Process in Multicultural Settings: Drawing on Student Perspectives." *Journal of Reading* 37 (May): 628–34.

Horn, M. 1999. *The World Encyclopedia of Comics.* Broomall, PA: Chelsea House.

Johnson, K. E. 1995. *Understanding Communication in Second Language Classrooms.* New York: Cambridge University Press.

Keene, E. O., and S. Zimmermann. 1997. *Mosaic of Thought: Teaching Comprehension in a Reader's Workshop.* Portsmouth, NH: Heinemann.

Krashen, S. 1982. *Principles and Practice in Second Language Acquisition.* New York: Pergamon Press.

———. 1985. *Inquiries and Insights: Second Language Teaching, Immersion and Bilingual Education, Literacy.* Hayward, CA: Alemany Press.

———. 1992. *Fundamentals of Language Education.* Beverly Hills, CA: Laredo.

———. 1993. *The Power of Reading: Insights from the Research.* Englewood, CO: Libraries Unlimited.

———. 1994. "Bilingual Education and Second Language Acquisition Theory." In *Schooling and Language Minority Students: A Theoretical Framework,* 2d ed., edited by C. F. Leyba, 47–75. Los Angeles: Evaluation, Dissemination and Assessment Center, California State University.

———. 2003. *Explorations in Language Acquisition and Use.* Portsmouth, NH: Heinemann.

Long, M. 1983. "Does Second Language Instruction Make a Difference? A Review of the Research." *TESOL Quarterly* 14 (1): 378–90.

Mayfield, M., J. Mayfield, and A. D. Genestre. 2001. "Strategic Insights from the International Comic Book Industry: A Comparison of France, Italy, Japan, Mexico, and the U.S.A." *American Business Review* 19 (June): 82–92.

McGroarty, M. 1993. "Cooperative Learning and Second Language Acquisition." In *Cooperative Learning: A Response to Cultural and Linguistic Diversity,* edited by D. Holt. Washington, DC: Center for Applied Linguistics.

Morrison, T. G., G. Bryan, and G. W. Chilcoat. 2002. "Using Student-Generated Comic Books in the Classroom." *Journal of Adolescent and Adult Literacy* 45 (May): 758–67.

Norton, B. 2003. "The Motivating Power of Comic Books: Insights from Archie Comic Readers." *The Reading Teacher* 57 (October): 140–47.

Palincsar, A. S., and A. L. Brown. 1984. "Reciprocal Teaching of Comprehension-Fostering and Comprehension-Monitoring Activities." *Cognition and Instruction* 1: 117–75.

Peyton, J. K., and L. Reed. 1990. *Dialogue Journal Writing with Nonnative English Speakers: A Handbook for Teachers.* Alexandria, VA: Teachers of English to Speakers of Other Languages.

Peyton, J. K., and J. Staton. 1996. *Dialogue Journals in the Multilingual Classroom: Building Language Fluency and Writing Skills Through Written Interaction.* Norwood, NJ: Ablex.

Rhode, M., and J. Bullough. 2003. Comics Research Bibliography. Accessed at *www.rpi.edu/~bulloj/comxbib.html.*

Rubenstein, A. 1998. *Bad Language, Naked Ladies, and Other Threats to the Nation: A Political History of Comic Books in Mexico.* Durham, NC: Duke University Press.

Russikoff, K. A., and J. L. Pilgreen. 1994. "Shaking the Tree of 'Forbidden Fruit': A Study of Light Reading." *Reading Improvement* 31 (summer): 122–24.

Schifini, A. 1988. *Sheltered English: Content Area Instruction for Limited English Proficient Students.* Downey, CA: Los Angeles County Office of Education.

Schulz, C. M. 1994. *Around the World in 45 Years: Charlie Brown's Anniversary Celebration.* Kansas City, MO: Andrews and McMeel.

Smith, F. 1997. *Reading Without Nonsense.* 3d ed. New York: Teachers College Press.

———. 2003. *Unspeakable Acts, Unnatural Practices: Flaws and Fallacies in "Scientific" Reading Instruction.* Portsmouth, NH: Heinemann.

Swain, E. H. 1978. "Using Comic Books to Teach Reading and Language Arts." *Journal of Reading* 22 (December): 253–58.

Swain, M. 1985. "Communicative Competence: Some Roles of Comprehensible Output in Its Development." In *Input in Second Language Acquisition,* edited by S. Gass and C. Madden, 235–53. Rowley, MA: Newbury House.

Sylwester, R. 1995. *A Celebration of Neurons: An Educator's Guide to the Human Brain.* Alexandria, VA: Association for Supervision and Curriculum Development.

Ujiie, J., and S. Krashen. 1996. "Comic Book Reading, Reading Enjoyment, and Pleasure Reading Among Middle Class and Chapter 1 Middle School Students." *Reading Improvement* 33 (spring): 51–54.

Vygotsky, L. S. 1978. *Mind in Society: The Development of Higher Psychological Processes.* Cambridge, MA: Harvard University Press.

Weiner, S. 2001. *The 101 Best Graphic Novels.* New York: NBM.

Wertham, F. 1954. *Seduction of the Innocent: The Influence of Comic Books on Today's Youth.* New York: Rinehart.

Williams, N. 1995. The Comic Book as Course Book: Why and How. Paper presented at the Annual Meeting of the Teachers of English to Speakers of Other Languages, Long Beach, California.

Wink, J. 2000. *Critical Pedagogy: Notes from the Real World,* 2d ed. New York: Allyn & Bacon.

Wolfe, P. 2001. *Brain Matters: Translating Research into Classroom Practice.* Alexandria, VA: Association for Supervision and Curriculum Development.

Worthy, J., M. Moorman, and M. Turner. 1999. "What Johnny Likes to Read Is Hard to Find in School." *Reading Research Quarterly* 34 (January/February/March): 12–27.

Wright, G. 1979. "The Comic Book: A Forgotten Medium in the Classroom." *Reading Teacher* 33: 158–61.

Wright, G., and R. Sherman. 1994. "What Is Black and White and Read All Over? The Funnies!" *Reading Improvement* 31 (spring): 37–47.

Wright, G., and R. Sherman. 1999. "Let's Create a Comic Strip." *Reading Improvement* 36 (summer): 66–72.

About the Author

Stephen Cary, a second language learner specialist, has worked as a teacher, resource teacher, and administrator. Dr. Cary currently consults in schools throughout the United States and abroad and serves as adjunct faculty in the University of San Francisco's teacher education and international-multicultural education programs. He is the author of *Working with Second Language Learners: Answers to Teachers' Top Ten Questions*, also from Heinemann and can be reached by email at <*stephencary@earthlink.net*>.

Index